THE PAGEANT OF HERALDRY

PLATE I

Frontispiece

ST. GEORGE AND THE DRAGON

*From a 15th Century French Manuscript
in the Bodleian Library.*

THE
PAGEANT OF HERALDRY

An Explanation of its Principles
&
its Uses To-day

COL. H. C. B. ROGERS, O.B.E.

With an Introduction
by
COL. H. A. B. LAWSON

ROTHSAY HERALD
&
LYON CLERK

PITMAN PUBLISHING CORPORATION
NEW YORK

Printed in Great Britain

CONTENTS

ILLUSTRATIONS

FIGURES IN THE TEXT

To my Wife

FOREWORD

HERALDRY, or Armory to give it its more ancient name, has from the beginning of time fascinated the minds of men. Firstly as a mere decorative art, then with its Standards and Banners it was from Biblical times a useful means of recognition—"Every man of the children of Israel shall pitch by his own standard, with the ensign of their fathers' house" (Numbers, chap. 2, verse 2). Finally in the twelfth century it emerged as a serious science of hereditary marks of recognition and distinction and of honour.

In the seventeenth, eighteenth and nineteenth, centuries it acquired a fashion value and suffered much from its would-be friends. A man who would cheerfully disclaim a knowledge of Engineering, Medicine or Law by saying his calling was other than that of an Engineer, a Doctor or a Lawyer yet felt that to avow an ignorance of Heraldry was to brand himself an ill-educated nobody.

To meet the demand a spate of writers poured out a cascade of volumes, and by making impossible claims for their subject and assigning fanciful Coats of Arms to the Biblical Kings and even to the Twelve Apostles did much to discredit the subject as a serious science.

Scotland was fortunate in having Sir George Mackenzie of Rosehaugh, the same who as King's Advocate so relentlessly prosecuted the Covenanters as to earn himself the appellation "Bloody Mackenzie" (his *Science of Herauldric* published 1680 still remains a monumental classic of the science); also Alexander Nisbit, whose 1722 edition of *Heraldry* is well worth perusal. England, of course, had her Sir William Dugdale, but generally speaking the standard was such that "The Preacher" might well bewail "And further, by these, my son, be admonished: of making many books there is no end; and much study is a weariness of the flesh". (Ecclesiastes, chap. 12, verse 12).

The present century has seen a revival of Scholarship, and Colonel H. C. B. Rogers's *The Pageant of Heraldry* is an excellent contribution in the best tradition; meticulously accurate, it covers an immense range for so small a volume and is admirably arranged. He is perhaps over-generous in Plate 11, facing page 70, in saying "the cadency differencing scheme *devised* by Mr. Stodart", who certainly classified and enlarged

13

it; but the system of bordures was established in Scottish Heraldry long before his time.

The Pageant of Heraldry it may confidently be predicted will weary no flesh, and Colonel Rogers has made students of Heraldry his debtors.

H. A. B. LAWSON,
Rothesay Herald.

ACKNOWLEDGEMENTS

In the writing of this book much help has been given by many people. I am indebted, in particular to Sir Christopher Lynch-Robinson for his kindly advice and assistance; to Mr. M. R. Trappes-Lomax, Somerset Herald, for his invaluable help; Mr. Gerard Slevin, Assistant Chief Herald of Ireland, for his patient and cheerful investigations into many questions; Mr. R. H. Jenkinson of the Belfast Central Library for his enthusiastic help; the Rev. P. H. Malden of the Roman Catholic Diocese of Southwark for his willing and cheery assistance; Imperial Chemical Industries for their beautiful book, the *Colour of Chivalry*; Mr. H. R. McIntosh, Mechanical Engineer of the Great Northern Railway (Ireland), for his kind gift of a transfer of the Railway's Armorial achievement; the Bodleian Library for permission to publish the illustration of St. George and the Dragon; Mr. A. L. Kipling of Messrs. Gale & Polden for his generous help and kindness in providing the beautiful plate of colours of the British Army; Mr. A. S. White, F.R.Hist.S., Hon. Secretary of the Society for Army Historical Research, for his ready help; Miss C. M. Egan, Hon. Secretary of the Heraldry Society and editor of the *Coat of Arms*, for the loan of blocks for illustrations and for her speedy response to appeals for assistance; Lt.-Colonel E. K. Walkington, Mr. Adrian Lynch-Robinson, and Major P. M. Marjoribanks-Egerton, M.B.E., the Royal Irish Fusiliers, for the valued loan of books; Colonel L. I. Cowper, O.B.E., D.L., for information, help and advice; Major J. B. Underwood, the King's Own Royal Regiment for his kind assistance; Miss J. D. Long for the many hours she has spent in typing this book, and last but by no means least, Sergeant O'Donoghue, late of the Royal Irish Constabulary, who presides with such loving care over the heraldic museum in Dublin Castle.

Chapter I

INTRODUCTORY

ANKIND has a love of symbols. It is a love which dates back to the first rude device erected as a tribal emblem, and which is typified to-day by such things as national flags, political badges, the colours and standards of the Army, trade marks (the modern descendants of the old "Merchants' Marks") and, finally, armorial achievements. Although this fondness for pictorial or sculptured signs is of such ancient origin, it was not till the first half of the twelfth century that the ordered and hereditary system which we call Heraldry, or more properly Armory, really started.

Many writers have attempted to prove that the science of Armory was practised by the ancient Greeks, the Egyptians and the Assyrians. A Scottish author of the seventeenth century went so far as to state that "Arms took their origin from the Example of the Patriarch Jacob, who, blessing his sons, gave them marks of distinction, which the twelve tribes bore on their Ensigns." At first sight there appears to be a certain amount of evidence in favour of these opinions. There are many descriptions in the works of the poets Aeschylus and Virgil, for instance, of the devices which their warriors bore on shield and helmet, and these devices are frequently heraldic in character, but there is no proof that any of these early emblems either followed a definite system or were hereditary, and they should be regarded as the predecessors of Armory rather than its ancestors. In much closer relationships to them are heraldic badges and the non-heraldic symbols which are in such common use at the present day. The famous Bayeux tapestry is evidence that no ordered heraldic system existed as late as the Norman Conquest, for although many of the most important personages are repeated several times, in no instance is any one of them depicted twice bearing the same device on his shield.

As late, then, as the eleventh century, and probably the first half of the twelfth, men certainly decorated their shields and accoutrements, but there were no rules regarding the emblems which they should display, or even preventing them from changing them as their fancy dictated. It is not known how the present heraldic system started or what caused its almost simultaneous appearance all over Western Europe. But there were probably three main factors which were responsible for its rapid growth in popularity. Firstly, feudal society was based on a close relationship between land tenure and the personal service in war which a man owed to his lord, from whom he held his land. It was an obvious advantage for a lord to have a permanent personal device by which his followers would know him in battle. The advent of a helm which completely obscured his features would accentuate that advantage. Secondly, the Crusades, with their tremendous emotional impact, invested armour and weapons with an almost religious significance. One can visualise a man's pride in the emblems under which he had fought in the holy wars and a son's ambition to prove himself worthy of his father's sword and device. Thirdly, the pageantry of that immensely popular mediaeval sport, the tournament, would have encouraged the adoption of personal devices by which their owners might be readily identified in the great European contests.

By the middle of the thirteenth century, at the latest, heraldry was firmly established in England with a set of rules and a technical language of its own. The Lions of England, in the form and colour in which they are depicted in the Royal Arms to-day, were already familiar throughout the civilised world, for they had been borne, probably, before the end of the Third Crusade and flaunted in the face of almost every monarch in Europe by that gallant, quarrelsome and enchanting knight-errant, King Richard I.

THE ACHIEVEMENT OF ARMS

The terms " Heraldry" and "Armory" are somewhat loosely used. "Heraldry", to be strictly accurate, includes everything within the province of the College of Arms; that is, arms, pedigrees, ceremonials, etc. "Armory" is concerned only with arms. An "Achievement of Arms" means the shield of arms and all the accessories which go with it. "Coat of Arms" is often used with the same meaning, but since it is derived from a garment worn over armour and embroidered with the arms, it is probably more correctly used in reference to the shield of arms alone.

To the uninitiated, the "Achievement" can be a very puzzling thing. Bad drawing and representation and the habit of sometimes leaving out one or more of the accessories are partly to blame. The Royal Arms are a case in point. Their representation includes almost every possible combination from the shield surmounted by a crown to an affair of lion, unicorn and tattered drapery with nothing else distinguishable. Sometimes, even, the lion and unicorn, ceasing their aggressive attitude, lie quietly down amidst assorted foliage and peer coyly at each other round the shield.

Once the construction of the achievement is understood, however, the correct emphasis on and representation of the component parts are readily appreciated. The normal achievement comprises essentially the shield, the helm and the mantling. To these may be added crest, wreath or crest coronet, motto, insignia of an order of knighthood, supporters, coronet of rank, compartment and insignia of office. These matters will be dealt with in detail in subsequent chapters, but their places in the achievement are outlined briefly below in order to give the reader a view of the wood before he becomes immersed in a study of the trees.

Fig. I.—THE ACHIEVEMENT OF A PEER
The Arms of the Duke of Norfolk

The Shield

The shield, or "escutcheon" as it is alternatively called, is the most important part of the achievement. It is, in fact, the basis of the whole thing, for it bears the arms to which everything else in the achievement is an accessory, and without which none of these accessories can exist.

The Helm

The shield, in the complete achievement, is surmounted by a helm. The type of helm and its position (that is, whether it is shown facing the observer or in profile) indicate the rank of the bearer of the arms.

The Crest

The term "crest" is the most abused in heraldry. It is commonly used, even by otherwise well-informed journals, to denote every kind of heraldic and non-heraldic device from the complete achievement to military badges. It is, in fact, an emblem which was worn on the helm, and it is so placed in the achievement. It is to be noted that a crest accompanies arms and is never granted by itself.

The Wreath

The wreath is a piece of twisted material which was placed round the helm to conceal the joint of crest and helm. It is shown on top of the helm and below the crest with six alternately coloured twists. Where the crest is shown apart from the achievement it is customary for it to be accompanied by the wreath.

In cases where a crest is shown on a coronet or crown, a wreath is not necessary, though it is in fact sometimes granted.

The Mantling

From the back of the helm is suspended a piece of material which is frequently shown as torn, and the ragged pieces blown into a decorative pattern. It has its origin on the piece of cloth which hung down to shield the back of the head and neck from the effects of a burning Eastern sun on the unprotected metal of the helm.

Insignia of an Order of Knighthood

Every possessor of any grade of an order of knighthood is entitled to display some insignia with his armorial achievement. This may take the form of a circlet of some description round the shield or merely a badge suspended below it. Baronets and knights-bachelor, too, have their own particular devices.

Coronets

A peer of the realm places his coronet above his shield. The helm, in this case, rests on top of the coronet.

Supporters

Certain persons and corporate bodies are entitled to supporters. These appear in various guises, but generally take the form of a pair of human beings or beasts supporting the shield on either side.

PLATE 2

ACHIEVEMENT OF A CADET OF ROGERS OF LANKE AND PENROSE IN CORNWALL

This family does not possess a crest. Note the use of metal on metal to show that the crescent is a mark of cadency.

The Compartment

To avoid the appearance of being suspended in mid-air the supporters must have something to stand on. This is known as the compartment. It may be a grassy mound, a rock, the sea, a stone platform, a gilded scroll (frequently known as a "gas-bracket") or the motto scroll.

The Motto

If there is a motto it is generally shown on a scroll beneath the arms, except in Scottish arms, where it is more often found above the crest.

Fig. II.—THE ACHIEVEMENT OF A PEER
The Arms of the Duke of Somerset

Insignia of Office

Certain appointments carry insignia of office, which are placed behind the arms. Examples of these are the crosiers of a bishop, the black-tipped gold batons of the Earl Marshal and the white wand of the Hereditary Lord Great Seneschal of Ireland.

Robe of Estate and Pavilion

The robe of estate of a peer is sometimes seen used as a background to his arms. This should not be confused with the pavilion, which is a tent-like background peculiar to Continental heraldry.

Examples of complete achievements are illustrated.

PLATE 3

A MEDIAEVAL MEMORIAL

Sir William Fitz Ralph, A.D. 1323—a Memorial in Pebmarsh Church, Essex. (After Waller.) Note: The Mixture of Mail and Plate Armour. The Coif or hood. The Plate protection for arms and legs. The Ornamental knee guards. The Plate discs for protection of shoulders and elbows. The surcoat divided at the front and back. The Arms displayed on shield alone.

Chapter II

ARMOUR

"That these Ensigns of Honour, as are commonly called ARMES which of later times have been chiefly used for distinction of families had their original from the practise of great Commanders in War, is not unknown to the learned: for certain it is, that the faces of all great Military Officers, being obscured by such Hoods and Helmets as were anciently worn in times of Battle: it was expedient, that by some other means their persons should be notified to their friends and followers. Necessity, therefore requiring it, they depicted upon their shields as also upon their Surcotes of Silke, Banners, Penons, &c., certain Badges, that might make them known at a distance from each other. . . . But these later times having devised other sorts of armour and weapons, both for offence and defence then of old were used: those marks and badges in Shields, Surcotes, &c., have been for divers past ages, as to any such military purpose, totally layed aside; and since merely retained as honourary Ensignes by the Nobility and Gentry."—*The Antient Usage in bearing of Arms*, by Sir WILLIAM DUGDALE, Garter Principal King of Arms, 1681.

WE have already touched briefly on the display of the "Honourary Ensignes", and to provide the necessary background for their more detailed consideration it would be well to acquire some slight acquaintance with their use in war and play before "these later times devised other sorts of armour and weapons".

Armour

Up till the last days of the Anglo-Saxon régime the usual protective clothing seems to have been quilted linen or leather. This was superseded by a leather foundation on which first scales of metal (scale armour) and later rings of metal (ringed armour) were sewn. The next step was chain mail, which in its final form covered the whole person of the wearer with its interlocking iron rings. It comprised a mail shirt, called a "hauberk"; a "coif", or hood covering the head; mail sleeves terminating in mittens; and mail stockings. Under the hauberk was a quilted tunic.

Although chain mail provided a very efficient protection against a sword, it was not so effective against a blow with a heavy weapon, and it was not long before parts of the body were additionally protected. By the middle of the twelfth century knees were sometimes protected by boiled leather or metal plates and a sort of metal shin-guard was in use between knee and ankle. Later other plates were introduced to protect the arms and shoulders. Finally mail became almost covered with plate and eventually gave place to full plate armour. Chain mail had a very long life, though. As late as the first half of the thirteenth century there are examples of chain mail being worn without any extra plate protection, and plate armour does not seem to have completely replaced mail until the early years of the fifteenth century.

From the first half of the thirteenth century a loose flowing garment, known as a surcoat, was worn over armour. It served the dual purpose of shielding the metal from the heat of the sun and of giving a degree of protection against rust. The surcoat was frequently charged with its owner's arms, and the term "coat of arms" was probably derived from it (though some authorities ascribe its origin to the tabard). The surcoat was slit below the waist in front and at the back for riding. In the latter half of the fourteenth century it was replaced by the jupon. The jupon was short and originally loose fitting, but was soon made to fit closely to the body. It appears to have been embroidered invariably with its owner's arms, and its close fit gave the wearer a very neat and smart appearance. Early in the fifteenth century the jupon was discarded and plate armour was worn uncovered until the introduction of the tabard about forty years later. The tabard was a short garment with very wide sleeves, and the arms were embroidered on the front and back of it and on each sleeve.

THE HELM

Men of rank in the later Anglo-Saxon period wore a conical metal cap. Shortly before the Norman Conquest a "nasal" or nose piece was fitted. This was a fairly wide metal tongue projecting downwards from the front of the cap and covering the nose. With this cap was worn a hood, or coif, which was originally of quilted material but ultimately chain mail. The hood covered the whole head under the metal cap and also the chin, so that with hood and nasal piece there was little of the face left exposed. This is the type of headgear which was worn by both sides at the Battle of Hastings, as can be seen from the Bayeux tapestry, though some patterns of hood do not appear to have covered the chin. There was no further alteration until the end of the twelfth century, when the conical cap was replaced by an improved model known as the "chapelle-de-fer". This was a flat-topped cylindrical affair with ear guards and nasal. The chapelle-de-fer had a short life and was succeeded by the "pot" or "barrel" helm. The barrel helm was worn over the coif and covered the whole head, but in its early form an opening was left for the features. This opening was sometimes covered by a movable visor and sometimes protected by a fixed nasal. In its later form the barrel

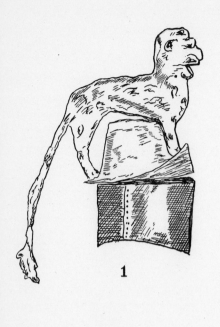

1

2

3

4

Fig. III.—Helms

No. 1. *Helm from the funeral armour of the Black Prince preserved in Canterbury Cathedral. The lion crest is made of cuirbouilli, faced with gesso and gilded. The crown of the chapeau was painted red with little roses and diapers of red and white.*

No. 2. *Great helm from brass of Sir William Staunton, 1326.*

No. 3. *Great helm with crest and mantling from brass of Sir John Daubeny, 1346.*

No. 4. *Fifteenth-century tilting helm.*

helm was a strong and heavy inverted pot with slits for the eyes and perforations for breathing through. It was made in a number of different shapes and was constructed either of metal or boiled leather (cuirbouilli) a very hard substance. The barrel helm was apparently an unsteady sort of headwear, for it was attached to its owner by a short chain, on the same principle, presumably, as the attachment of a hunting-bowler.

Towards the end of the thirteenth century there were two important innovations. The first of these was the "great" helm, which rested on the shoulders and was secured front and back. The second was the "bascinet". This was originally a hemispherical metal cap which was worn over the coif as an additional protection to the head when the knight was not engaged in actual battle and was carrying his great helm. The bascinet was gradually enlarged to give protection to the neck, and about the middle of the fourteenth century the coif was replaced by a "camail" or mail curtain which was laced to the bottom of the bascinet, covered the chin and spread out over the shoulders. The great helm was still worn over bascinet and camail when in close contact with the enemy. It was, however, a heavy and clumsy gear, and various hinged plates or visors were fixed to the bascinet itself in an attempt to dispense with the great helm altogether. None of these were very successful until, about the end of the fourteenth century, the so-called "pig-faced" bascinet was produced with a large snout-shaped visor. A high steel collar was added to this in replacement of the camail. The great helm was now used only for jousting and was frequently fitted with large crests made from cuirbouilli. At the time that experiments with visors were being made with the bascinet, development was proceeding along an entirely different line. The "schallern" was a metal hat with a long curving back-piece to protect the neck. It was not unlike certain patterns of firemen's helmets, except that it came very low over the nose and a slit was provided for the eyes. It was thus a combined helmet and visor, for it could be pushed upward on to the back of the head. With the schallern was worn a lower face-piece which protected the chin and throat. The pig-faced bascinet and the schallern were the most popular fighting-helms until about the middle of the fifteenth century.

In the meantime, from the great helm were derived three different kinds of helm to serve the several purposes of the tournament. The joust-ing type, used for individual mounted combat, was a strong, beautifully shaped helm securely bolted to the cuirass, with an eye-slit high up towards the crown so that its wearer could only see out when he was leaning forward in the saddle for the attack. This is probably the most popular type for use in heraldic achievements where a closed visor is specified. For foot combat a round-shaped helm was used. It was also

PLATE 4

A MEDIAEVAL MEMORIAL

Sir John Wingfield, c. A.D. 1400—a Memorial in Letheringham Church, Suffolk. (From Boutell.) Note: The Bascinet and Camail. The Mail Hauberk and Plate Armour. The Close-fitting Jupon embroidered with Arms. The Misericorde, or Dagger. The Short Sword.

called a bascinet and had a visor perforated with a large number of holes to enable its wearer to see in any direction. The third type was the so-called "tournament" helm, used for the tourney or mêlée, which was fought with sword and mace. It was similar to the bascinet, but had either a barred visor or bars riveted to the helm, or, occasionally, wire-mesh protection.

There was another revolution in design about 1440, when the Italians produced the "armet". This was a round helm with a visor. The lower part opened on hinges and allowed a close fitting to the head. Its weight was carried by a steel collar or "gorget". The armet is a suitable design for heraldic use when a helm is required with an open visor.

Another type of contest in the tournament—a mounted affair with wooded clubs as weapons—was responsible for the introduction of a round helm with a grid-iron or lattice-work protected opening.

The last helm which should be mentioned is the "buckler". This was another round pattern with the face-opening protected by vertical bars or grills. It was often made of gilded leather and was only used for ceremonial purposes and for funerals. This is the helm which is represented in heraldic drawings when a barred type is required.

THE TOURNAMENT

The nearest modern spectacular equivalent to a mediaeval tournament would be something between a County Show and an Athletic Meeting, and it probably aroused as much excitement and enthusiasm as a Wembley Cup Final. On the ground where the tournament was to be held would be a mass of gay tented pavilions. A large covered pavilion was erected for the ladies, who played an important part at tournaments, and each knight had his own richly decorated pavilion above which flew his banner emblazoned with his arms. The arena where the contests took place, known as the "lists", was bordered by galleries, brilliant with colour and badges, for the use of the more illustrious of the spectators of both sexes. The size of the lists probably varied considerably, but those prepared at Smithfield under the instructions of King Edward IV measured three hundred and seventy feet in length and two hundred and sixty feet in breadth. The knights started to arrive some days before the date fixed for the start of the tournament. They came not only from all parts of the British Isles but from most of the countries in Europe, each with his esquires, horses, armour, weapons, banners, horse trappings, etc. On arrival the heralds, who were responsible for the organisation of the tournament, examined each knight's credentials. On the day before the opening of the tournament the shields, helms and banners of the contestants were collected with much ceremony in one hall and arranged under the instructions of the Judges of the Tournament. The ladies were now officially conducted round, and might, by touching shield or crest, accuse the competitor of a fault or crime against chivalry. The unfortunate offender would be punished, executed or challenged to *combat à outrance* by one or more of the outraged lady's admirers, according to the magnitude of his offence and the custom of the tournament. The Chevalier d'honneur, the knight who was to attend the Lady of the Tournament, was next selected. His principal job was to extend the "Merci des Dames" when the Lady of the Tournament wished to forbid further attacks on a wounded or disabled knight. His helm and crest were handed over to the custody of the ladies for the duration of the tournament. Challenges might now be made by tapping the proposed opponent's shield with the weapon with which it was intended to fight; the heralds noting down the name of challenger and challenged. At some period it appears to have been the practice to hang up two different shields—one for peace and one for war; and according to which was tapped the contest was fought with blunt or sharp weapons.

The ceremonial practices and contests changed, of course, considerably over the six hundred odd years during which the tournament was the most popular sporting event in Europe; and it is only possible in this short outline to give a brief description of fairly typical organisation and events.

Mr. Jorrocks' famous description of hunting might be fairly given to the tournament: "The Sport of Kings, the image of war without its guilt, and only five-and-twenty per cent. of its danger." The thing was rough, but surprisingly few were killed. The contestants had stout armour, and great use was made of wooden weapons.

The tourney, or mêlée, was a team event. The opposing parties of knights entered the lists through barriers at opposite ends and rode round the arena several times, paying their respects to the King and the ladies. They then formed up, the Charge sounded and the teams galloped into the attack with wooden swords and maces. At the end of a battle, which might last for some hours, the victory was decided by the number on each side who had been unhorsed, and the Lady of the Tournament distributed the prizes.

Jousts were single combats and generally followed the mêlée. There were several kinds, but the two main varieties were the tilt and the free joust. The tilt itself was a wooden barrier about five feet in height over which the contending knights fought. Each knight kept the barrier on his left and endeavoured to unseat his opponent with a long blunt fir pole as they charged towards each other. In the free joust the barrier was dispensed with. Lances were used, generally tipped with a ferrule, but contests with sharp lances sometimes took place. Some questionable practices sometimes appear to have been used in jousting. An ancient account of a combat between Lord Scales and the so-called Bastard of Burgundy in the time of King Edward IV states that, "The Lord Scales, having a long spike fixed on his chaffron (pommel of his saddle) which as they enclosed, ran into the nostrils of the bastard's horse, by the anguish whereof, he reared himself with that violence, that he stumbled backwards, whereby his rider was unhorsed". Nobody seems to have thought that Lord Scales was breaking the rules, but then the Bastard seems to have been a little too overbearingly conceited with his prowess to be popular.

Various other contests took place both on foot and mounted. One of these, a mounted event called the "baston", was fought with wooden clubs; the object being the destruction of the opponents' crests. This seems to survive to-day (or did while the British Army still had horses) in a mounted combat in which the competitors wear fencing-masks with balloons tied closely to the top. The object, of course, is to break the balloon.

The pageantry and social side of these tournaments is well illustrated by the following account by Maitland (the ancient writer who has just been quoted) in his *History of London*: "King Richard II designing to hold a tournament at London on the Sunday after Michaelmas, sent divers heralds to make proclamations of it in all the principal Courts of Europe, and accordingly not a few princes, and great numbers of the prime nobility resorted hither from France, Germany, the Netherlands, etc. This solemnity began on Sunday afternoon, from the Tower of London, with a pompous cavalcade of sixty Ladies, each leading an armed Knight by a silver chain, being attended by their squires of honour, and passing through Cheapside, rode to Smithfield, where the Jousts and Tournaments continued several days with magnificent variety of entertainments; on which occasion the King kept open house at the Bishop of London's palace, for all persons of distinction, and every night concluded with a ball."

Chapter III

THE SHIELD

THE shield is, as has already been mentioned, the principal part of the armorial achievement. Its shape both in practical and armorial use has varied considerably. At the time of the Norman Conquest shields were long and narrow, and tapered to a sharp point, with a top which was sometimes curved and sometimes straight with curved corners. They were not flat but rounded horizontally to give greater protection to the body. The sharp end made it easy to drive the shield into the ground, and a line of shields so fixed provided an effective palisade for dismounted defence.

Shields were not normally made of metal, as is frequently supposed, but of wood covered with linen or leather and strengthened with metal bands or bosses. The leather was normally cuirbouilli, that is leather boiled in oil, made plastic by beating and then pressed into the required shape. When dry it was very hard. At about the end of the eleventh century, however, it does appear that shields were sometimes used with an all-metal and highly polished surface. This was probably a brief fashion.

There was little change in the Norman pattern of shield throughout the eleventh and twelfth centuries, and it was, therefore, the first on which proper arms were borne. About the middle of the twelfth century, however, a shorter shield began to make its appearance, and by the first half of the thirteenth century this had shrunk to the shape of an inverted equilateral arch, and the Norman shield had disappeared except for fighting on foot. The cause of this shortening of the shield was the improvement in armour, which was to result eventually in its total disappearance from the battlefield.

In the fourteenth century the only alteration in the shape of the shield was a gradual straightening of the sides, resulting firstly in the so-called "heater" shape (from its resemblance to a flat iron), and later to a pattern of which the sides were straight and at right angles to the top for about two-thirds of the height of the shield.

By the fifteenth century the use of plate armour was universal and the shield was only used at tournaments. According to Mr. G. W. Eve in his *Heraldry as an Art*, the last type to be used in war had a sharp central vertical ridge and round base. Tournament shields began to assume curious shapes, and contemporary heraldic drawings were an

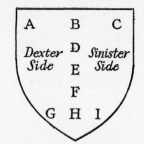

Points of the Escutcheon
ABC *the Chief*
D *the Honour Point*
E *the Fess Point*
F *the Nombril Point*
GHI *the Base*

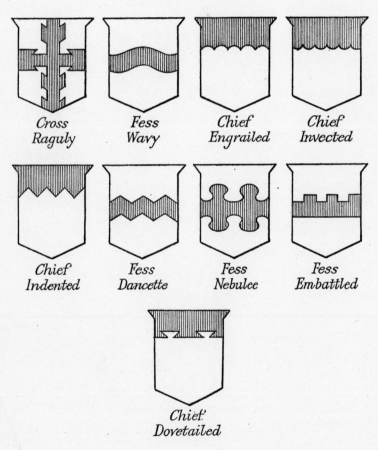

Fig. IV.—THE POINTS OF THE SHIELD AND THE PARTITION LINES

ornamental version of these. A favourite heraldic type in the fifteenth and sixteenth centuries was the cusped pattern; that is, with the border formed by a series of concave curves. Later varieties of the cusped form had a notch cut in the dexter chief. This was a representation of the tournament "à bouche" shield, which had a notch in the top right-hand side for the lance to pass through. An "à bouche" shield appears on one recent issue of the half-crown piece. The fifteenth century saw the first examples of a purely decorative shield with foliated or scrolled edges in heraldic drawings, and this shield became common in the sixteenth century. The cusped and foliated shields were generally of an attractive and artistic design and bore no relation to the appalling scroll-work of the later eighteenth and early nineteenth centuries. The most extraordinary Victorian shields were notable more for their background than their shape. A type regarded as suitable for eminent sailors, for instance, had a background of cannon, flags, masts and anchors all piled on a rock with the sea breaking at its foot.

The present tendency in heraldic design shows a return to simplicity and to boldness in execution—a trend which anyone may test for himself by comparing the design of the shield and its charges on successive issues of the half-crown piece.

It is probable that, in the case of shields in normal use, the arms were painted on them in flat colour. But at the same time the charges shown in the arms are intended to be three-dimensional and on shields intended for important ceremonial occasions they were represented in relief. These ceremonial shields were frequently beautiful examples of the shield-worker's art. The surface would be constructed of layers of canvas and leather stretched and glued to the framework. The charges would be modelled in cuirbouilli or some other suitable substance and pinned to the surface. Diapered patterns might then be punched on to the field of the shield before the gold, silver and colour were painted on.

THE POINTS OF A SHIELD

In order to be able to describe the position of charges, names have been given to the various parts of a shield and to nine specific points on its surface. These latter are known as the "points" of a shield. The whole of the area enclosed by the border of the shield is known as the "field". The right-hand side is the "dexter" and the left-hand side the "sinister"; but it is necessary to remember that right and left are so called from the point of view of the bearer of the shield. The dexter side is, therefore, on the left as one looks at it. The top of the shield is the "chief" and the bottom the "base". The chief is regarded as the most "honourable" of the four, and the order of precedence of the remainder is "dexter", "sinister", "base". The centre of the shield is known as the "fess point". There are three "chief" points; the "middle chief" point in the centre of an imaginary band across the top of the field, the "dexter chief" point at the dexter end of this band and the "sinister chief" point at the sinister end. Similarly there are three "base" points: "middle base", "dexter base" and "sinister base". The "honour point" lies between the middle chief point and the fess point, and is sometimes shown as being rather closer to the former. It is possibly so named as being the part of the shield which covers the heart. The "nombril point" is between the fess point and the middle base point. The name is derived from "navel", the part of the anatomy which it might be expected to cover.

DIAPER

A very attractive method of enriching the surface of a shield known as "diapering" was frequently used in the Middle Ages and is still used in some of the finest examples of heraldic art. It is purely ornamental and is used primarily to break up large flat surfaces which are bare of heraldic charges. The method of diapering depends on the surface being treated. In an armorial painting on paper or vellum, for instance, the design might be drawn in a darker or lighter shade of the colour used for the field of the shield.

THE TINCTURES

The tinctures used in English and Scottish armory are few and simple. They consist of "metals", "colours" and "furs". The two metals are gold and silver, known as "or" and "argent" respectively. In painting they may be, and frequently are, represented by yellow and white. There are five colours in normal use: red called "gules"; blue, "azure"; green, "vert"; purple, "purpure"; and black, "sable". There are two other colours which are very rarely encountered; these are "murray" or "sanguine", which is a reddish-purple, and "tenné", which is orange-tawny. They are commonly called "stains" owing to their supposed use in colouring abatements of honour, that is, marks of disgrace.

The archaic words used for the metals and colours are immediately derived from the old Norman-French, but some of them have an Eastern origin. They are pronounced as if they were English. (This rule applies to most of the Norman-French words used in heraldry, though there are some exceptions.) Argent, gules, azure, sable and purpure can be abbreviated arg., gu., az., sa. and purp. respectively.

At about the middle of the seventeenth century a system of hatching was selected by an Italian Jesuit, Fr. Francisco Di Petra Sancta, from a number of systems which had been used to represent the tinctures in black and white illustrations of achievements of arms. This method became standardised and is still in common use, though it does not appear ever to have had official sanction. The symbols used are as follows:

Or . . dots
Argent . the surface left plain
Gules . . perpendicular lines
Azure . . horizontal lines
Vert . . diagonal lines downward from dexter to sinister
Purpure . diagonal lines downward from sinister to dexter
Sable . . perpendicular and horizontal lines crossing each other
Murray . dexter and sinister diagonal lines crossing each other
Tenné. . horizontal and diagonal lines downward from sinister to dexter crossing each other

Any thing living or inanimate may be depicted in its natural colours, in which case it is described as "proper". Where, however, the term "proper" would not give a clear enough description owing to the object described existing in a number of colours (e.g. a bull), the actual colours intended may be stated.

There are two principal furs, "ermine" and "vair". Ermine is always shown as white covered with black spots, which represent the tails of the animal. Ermine has three variations. "Ermines" is its reverse, having white spots on black. "Erminois" consists of black spots on gold, and "pean" is the reverse of this, that is gold spots on black. It should be noted that ermine and ermines are always now represented as black and white, though at one time they were sometimes represented as black and silver.

Vair is the fur of a kind of squirrel which was blue-grey on top and white underneath. Vair was very popular as a lining of cloaks, and the skins when sewn together appeared as a series of alternating blue-grey and white cup-shaped patches. That it at one time had a wide use is shown by the well-known story of Cinderella, the ugly sisters, the Prince and the vair slippers (not "verre" or, in English, glass). As heraldically drawn, vair is represented by rows of little bell-shaped shields—blue shields which are upright, and silver or white ones which are upside down and fit into the spaces between the blue ones. (Some authorities think that these positions should be reversed.) Like ermine, vair has its variations. If tinctures other than silver and blue are used, the fur is known as "vairy", for instance, or and gules. In "counter-vair" the blue and silver panes are alternatively upright and upside down, so that the chiefs and bases

Colours

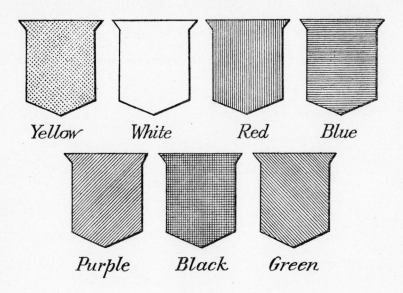

Yellow   White   Red   Blue

Purple   Black   Green

Fur

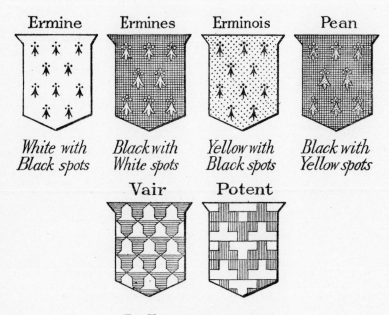

Ermine   Ermines   Erminois   Pean

White with   Black with   Yellow with   Black with
Black spots   White spots   Black spots   Yellow spots

Vair   Potent

Fig. V.—COLOURS AND FURS

of shields of the same tincture are in opposition. There are certain other varieties which are not seen very often. "Potent", another variety, is similar to vair except that the shield-shaped panes are replaced by blue and silver "potents" or crutch-shaped patches. It has come to be regarded as a separate fur, but originally it was merely a different way of drawing vair. Like vair, tinctures other than blue and silver must be specified; e.g. potent of or and gules. "Counter-potent" is the counterpart of counter-vair.

It is a rule in heraldry that colour may not be placed upon colour nor metal upon metal. The early herald-paynters sought to achieve designs which would be easy to identify at a distance. They used simple brilliant colours and they appreciated that for clarity an object placed on a coloured background must be of a metal, and vice versa. A design in which this rule is not observed always loses in sharpness of definition and general effect. The rule does not apply to a fur or "proper", since neither is a heraldic metal or colour. In the case of a field which is partly a metal and partly a colour, and has a charge resting on both parts, the rule is waived, since otherwise a charge of either a metal or a colour would be bound to transgress it. Apart from these, there are one or two minor exceptions to the colour rule which will be dealt with in due course.

The Arms of Jerusalem constitute a well-known breach of the colour rule. This is commonly supposed to have been deliberate in order that the Holy City's five gold crosses on a silver field should occupy a unique position in heraldry.

Chapter IV

THE HONOURABLE ORDINARIES, THE SUB-ORDINARIES AND PARTITIONING

THE so-called Honourable Ordinaries and Sub-Ordinaries are geometrical figures which are commonly used as charges on the shield. They have been in use from the earliest days of heraldry, but their exact origin is uncertain. It is possible that they are derived from the pieces of various shapes which were fixed across shields to strengthen them. It would be an obvious form of elementary decoration to colour such pieces differently to the remainder of the shield. Such decoration would be dependent, of course, on the form of strengthening used with the particular shield, and so there would be little permanence in design. In some cases, however, it may have become traditional for a family to use the same type of structure and the same decorative colours; and this traditional design, perhaps, eventually became the heraldic bearing of the family.

There is little to differentiate the honourable ordinaries (commonly called ordinaries) from the sub-ordinaries; but the former are all composed of broad bands which stretch across the field, whereas the latter are generally more complex or smaller figures. The honourable ordinaries are, as their name implies, the more important of the two.

The ordinaries and sub-ordinaries, like all other charges, are three-dimensional; that is, they are not merely painted on a shield but are considered to be solid objects which are placed on it. In addition to having plain edges, they may also have ornamental ones of various patterns. The lines which form these edges are also used to partition the field and are known as "partition lines".

The various methods by which a field can be partitioned are derived from and are generally named after one of the ordinaries or sub-ordinaries.

THE HONOURABLE ORDINARIES

There are usually considered to be seven (the perfect number) honourable ordinaries. They are:

The Bend	The Cross
The Chevron	The Fess
The Chief	The Pale
The Saltire	

PLATE 5

ORDINARIES

Fig. 1

CHIEF

John de Bicknore, c. Henry III, bore Argent, a chief azure.

Fig. 2

CHIEF INDENTED

Sir Roger Bownd, 1308, bore Argent, a chief indented sable.

Fig. 3

BEND

Richard le Scrope, c. Richard II, bore Azure, a bend or.

Fig. 4

BENDLETS ENHANCED

Nicholas Beron of Clacton, c. Edward IV, bore Argent, three bendlets enhanced gules.

Fig. 5

BENDY WAVY

Playter of Suffolk bear Bendy Wavy of six argent and azure.

Fig. 6

PALE

Baron Henry de L'Orti vel de Urtiaco, 1299, bore Vert, a pale or.

Fig. 7

PALLETS

— Rowthings, c. Edward III, bore Argent, four pallets gules.

Fig. 8

PALY

Sir Peers de Borgate, c. Edward II, bore Paly of six, argent and sable.

Fig. 9

PALY-BENDY

Buck, baronets of Lincolnshire, bear Paly-Bendy or and azure, a canton ermine.

Fig. 10

FESS

Sire Abbehall of Gloucestershire, c. Edward II, bore Or, a fess gules.

Fig. 11

FESS DANCETTE

Roger de Aston, c. Edward III, bore Argent, a fess dancette sable.

Fig. 12

FESS EMBATTLED

Richard Abberbury, c. Richard II, bore Or, a fess embattled sable.

Most of them have diminutives and varieties—a description of, firstly, the ordinaries and secondly, the diminutives and varieties are given below.

(a) *Ordinaries*

Bend. A broad diagonal band from the dexter chief to the sinister base. A band which runs from the sinister chief to the dexter base is called a "bend sinister".

Chevron. A figure shaped like an inverted V with the lower ends of the arms resting on the dexter and sinister base points. The position of the top of the chevron is not fixed, but it is normally placed as high as possible without cramping any other charges there may be on the shield.

Chief. A broad band across the top of the field, the upper edge of which coincides with the top edge of the shield. It is normally superimposed over the tressure and bordure (sub-ordinaries, qq.v.) when these appear in the field. It is not itself debruised or surmounted by any other ordinary unless one of these is added later as a mark of difference. It cannot be borne together with a fess. It has always been considered as the most honourable of the ordinaries. The chief is not bound by the tincture rule since it is a development of a field party per fess (q.v.) and can therefore be regarded as a partition of the field as well as an ordinary. It is not considered good heraldry, however, to ignore the rule.

Cross. The ordinary heraldic cross is a combination of the fess and the pale; that is, a vertical and a horizontal band intersecting and touching the edges of the field (i.e. it is a cross "throughout"). There are great numbers of varieties of cross, some of which are listed below.

Fess. A broad horizontal band across the middle of the field. It is only borne singly.

Pale. A broad vertical band down the middle of the field.

Saltire. The figure commonly known as St. Andrew's Cross; a combination of a bend and a bend sinister.

(b) *Diminutives, Varieties and Terms associated with Ordinaries*

Abased. Said of an ordinary (or other charge) which is placed below the normal position in the field (e.g. three bendlets abased).

Bar. A horizontal band which is narrower than a fess. It is not normally borne singly.

Bar Gemel. A pair of very narrow horizontal bands, each of which is narrower than a barrulet. Two pairs would be called "two bars gemel".

Barrulet. A horizontal band which is narrower than a bar.

Baston. A narrow bend. Synonymous with bendlet.

Baton. A bendlet sinister couped.

Bendlet. A narrow bend. Synonymous with baston.

Braced. A term applied to three chevronels placed side by side with arms interlaced.

Chevronel. A chevron with narrow arms.

Cost. A term sometimes applied in Scotland to a bendlet.

Cotised. A term applied to a fess, bar, bend, pale or chevron which has a very narrow diminutive of itself on each side. One of these ordinaries with two of these narrow stripes on each side is said to be "double cotised".

Couped. Said of an ordinary (except a chief) of which the extremities do not reach the edge of the field.

Crosslet. A little cross. In modern heraldry it often has an additional short arm across each limb.

Crusilly. Powdered with crosslets.

Dance. An ordinary which zigzags across the field is called "dancy" or "dancette" (e.g. a bend dancy). The term "dance" by itself is sometimes applied to a fess or bar dancy.

Enhance. Said of an ordinary (or other charge) which is placed above the normal position in the field (e.g. three bendlets enhanced).

Fillet. A fillet cross is one drawn throughout of very narrow width. It is sometimes used to make quarterings indivisible.

Fimbriated. A term applied to an ordinary (or other charge) which is edged with a metal or a colour to prevent two colours or two metals coming together. It occurs most often with a cross. For example, the azure field of the Union Flag is charged with the cross gules of St. George fimbriated argent. The tincture rule is thus preserved.

Fitchy. Applied to a cross which has the lower limb tapering to a point.

Floretty. A cross floretty has fleurs-de-lis issuing from the ends of the limbs.

Formy. A cross formy (sometimes called "patée") has spreading arms with square ends. The Victoria Cross (although officially and wrongly described as Maltese) is formy.

Patonce. A cross patonce has the end of its arms splayed into three points.

Position of Charges. A charge (such as a sword, for instance) may be placed in the direction of an ordinary. If in the horizontal position it would be termed "fesswise"; in the vertical, "palewise"; and diagonally, "bendwise". Two or more charges may be placed in relative positions to each other such as would be taken up by an ordinary. If vertically one below the other (like the lions in the Royal Arms of England) they are "in pale". Similarly they may be "in bend" or "in fess".

Potent. A cross potent has each of its limbs shaped like the letter T.

Saltonel. A little saltire.

Scarp. A name sometimes applied to a bend sinister.

Tau. A Tau cross is shaped like the letter T; that is, with no upper limb.

Voided. Applied to an ordinary (or other charge) from which the centre has been removed so that the field shows through.

THE SUB-ORDINARIES

The sub-ordinaries are generally considered to number fourteen, or twice the perfect number. They are:

The Annulet	The Inescutcheon
The Billet	The Label
The Bordure	The Lozenge
The Canton	The Orle
The Flaunch	The Pile
The Fret	The Roundel
The Gyron	The Tressure

41

PLATE 6

ORDINARIES

Fig. 1
FESS COTISED
Henry Bishopbury, c. Edward III, bore Argent, a fess double cotised sable.

Fig. 2
BARS WAVY
Sir William Basset of Tehidy, Cornwall, c. Edward III, bore Or, three bars wavy gules.

Fig. 3
BARS GEMEL
John Barry, c. Edward III, bore Gules, two bars gemel argent.

Fig. 4
QUARTERLY
William de Burgh, c. Henry III, bore Quarterly or and azure.

Fig. 5
CHEVRON
John Trelawney, c. Edward I, bore Argent, a chevron sable.

Fig. 6
CHEVRONELS
John de Sutton bore, at the second Dunstable tournament 1334. Or, three chevronels sable.

Fig. 7
CROSS
Walter de Burgh, Earl of Ulster, c. Edward III, bore Or, a cross gules. The ancient arms of Bigod, Earl of Norfolk.

Fig. 8
CROSS PATONCE
William le Latimer of Corby, banneret, bore, at the battle of Falkirk 1298 and at the Siege of Carlaverock 1300, Gules, a cross patonce or. Latimer was a Crusader.

Fig. 9
SALTIRE
John Gage, c. Henry IV, bore Per saltire argent and azure, a saltire gules.

Fig. 10
PILE
Sir Francis Aldam of Kent, c. Edward II, bore Azure, a pile or.

Fig. 11
PILES IN POINT
Rauf Basset, c. Henry III, bore Or, three piles in point gules.

Fig. 12
SHAKEFORK
Cunningham of Scotland bear Argent, a shakefork sable.

Only the flaunch has a diminutive and only the fret, lozenge and roundel have varieties. Their sub-ordinaries and their diminutives are listed below.

(a) *The Sub-Ordinaries*

Annulet. A ring. Annulets are sometimes interlaced. Three annulets interlaced, two in chief and one in base, are a sign of the Holy Trinity.

Billet. A rectangular figure borne with the long sides vertical. It is seldom seen singly and occurs most often as "billety"; that is, a field powdered with billets.

Bordure. A band which is placed round the field with its outer edge coinciding with the outer edge of the shield. It is not bound by the tincture rule.

Canton. A square figure placed, with rare exceptions, in the dexter chief corner of the field. It surmounts every other charge except a bordure when the latter is used as a mark of cadency or difference. If it has been subsequently added to the arms (e.g. to carry an augmentation), it need not conform to the tincture rule.

Flaunch. Flaunches are always borne in pairs. They consist of segments of circles of large diameter projecting into the field from the dexter and sinister sides.

Fret. A mascle (q.v.) interlaced by a bendlet and a bendlet sinister.

Gyron. A triangular figure. (Two of them would be formed by a line in bend crossing a line in fess.) It is seldom borne singly.

Inescutcheon. A small shield borne as a charge.

Label. A narrow bar in chief with three or five rectangular pendants. It is generally now used as a mark of cadency. When borne as a charge it usually extends right across the field. As a cadency mark, it may be couped. Its origin is unknown, but there is an effigy at Artois of Charles Count D'Eu which has a collar consisting of, apparently, a narrow cord from which is suspended a series of strips, like the pendants of a label, charged with castles. It may therefore have been a mark of favour or distinction.

Lozenge. A figure which is the same shape as the diamond in a pack of cards.

Orle. A band which follows the outline of the shield but does not touch its edges.

Pile. A triangular wedge-shaped figure issuing from the chief, unless otherwise described. A single pile can issue from any point of the field except the base (as the field would then be described as "per chevron"). Two issuing in chief and one in base are, however, quite frequently seen. When three piles issue from the middle, dexter and sinister chief, and the three points nearly meet about the nombril or middle base point, they are described as "three piles in point".

Roundel. A small circular disc. Although it can be described as a "roundel gules", etc., if it is of a single metal or colour, or barry wavy argent and azure, it is more usually given one of the special names listed under the varieties.

Tressure. Shaped like a narrow orle and always borne double and ornamented with fleurs-de-lis, the heads of which are turned outwards and inwards alternately. The stems of the fleurs-de-lis do not appear between the two tressures. As such it is known as the "double tressure flory-counter-flory" and is peculiar to Scottish heraldry. It may not be granted to any person without the express licence of the Sovereign. (There is one example of a plain single tressure in British heraldry and one of a plain double one; both of which were granted by King James V of Scotland.) Except for the chief and the canton, all ordinaries and sub-ordinaries are enclosed by a tressure and are not continued beyond its inner edge.

(b) *Diminutives and Varieties*

Bezant.   A gold roundel. It derives its name from a coin of Byzantium. Three bezants were part of the arms of Lombardy and were anciently used by the bankers of that country as a device—hence the pawnbroker's three golden balls.

Flasque.   A diminutive of a flaunch. Flasques also are borne in pairs.

Fountain.   A roundel barry wavy argent and azure.

Fretty.   A field covered with bendlets and bendlets sinister interlacing in the form of a lattice work.

Fusil.   Similar to a lozenge but narrower; that is, with more acute angles at the top and bottom.

Golpe.   A purple roundel, sometimes referred to as a "wound".

Hurt.   A blue roundel. It represents the fruit of that name.

Mascle.   A lozenge voided.

Pellet.   A black roundel which often represents a canon ball.

Plate.   A silver roundel which has its origin in a silver coin.

Pomme.   A green roundel representing, as its name implies, an apple. It is sometimes called a "pomeis" in the singular only.

Rustre.   A lozenge with a round hole in the middle.

Syke.   Another name for a fountain (q.v.).

Torteaux.   A red roundel.

Trellis.   Similar to fretty, but the bendlets are all on top of the bendlets sinister and are nailed to them, or "cloué" at the junctions. The colour of the nails is specified (e.g. a trellis gu. cloué arg.).

PARTITIONING

The following are the principle methods of partitioning the field; that is, dividing its surface into areas of different tinctures:

Barruly.   Divided into an even number of more than ten bar-like sections or "pieces" (e.g. barruly or and azure).

Barry.   Divided into an even number of ten or less bar-like pieces (e.g. barry of six pieces argent and azure or, merely, barry of six argent and azure). The number of pieces is specified.

Barry-Bendy.   Divided into sections formed by intersecting barry and bendy lines.

Bendy.   Divided into an even number of bend-like pieces. The number of pieces is specified.

Chequy.   Divided into small squares by barry and paly lines (e.g. chequy or and gules).

Chevronny.   Divided into an even number of chevron-like pieces. The number of pieces is specified.

Gobony.   An ordinary divided into one row of rectangular blocks of alternating tinctures. "Counter-gobony" is similar, but consists of two rows. (Sometimes the terms "company" and "counter-compony" are used.)

Gyronny.   Divided both quarterly and per saltire into eight gyron-like sections. It may be divided into more or less sections, but in that case the number must be specified (e.g. gyronny of ten or and vert).

Lozengy.—Divided into lozenge-like sections by a series of lines in bend and bend sinister crossing each other.

PLATE 7

ORDINARIES

Fig. 1
GYRONNY
Sir John Bassingbourne, c. Edward II, bore Gyronny or and gules.

Fig. 2
ANNULETS
Henry Lowther, c. Edward III, bore Argent, six annulets sable.

Fig. 3
BORDURE
Sire de Hundescote, c. Edward I, bore Ermine, a bordure gules.

Fig. 4
FRETTY
John de Cokesalton, c. Henry III, bore Argent, fretty gules.

Fig. 5
LOZENGES
Sir William Montagu, baron, bore at first Dunstable tournament 1308, Argent, three lozenges conjoined in fess gules.

Fig. 6
FUSIL
Richard Dautrey, c. Edward III, bore Or, five fusils conjoined in fess sable.

Fig. 7
MASCLES
Sir Stephen de Brielmanstone, c. Edward II, bore Argent, seven mascles conjoined sable.

Fig. 8
ORLE
Sir John de Laundeles, c. Edward III, bore Azure, an orle or.

Fig. 9
ROUNDELS
Sir Alan la Zoinhe of Ashby, bore at the Battle of Falkirk 1298, Gules, ten bezants, 4, 3, 2, 1.

Fig. 10
LOZENGY
Thomas de Warbleton, c. Henry III, bore Lozengy, or and azure.

Fig. 11
FRET
John Salkeld, c. Edward I, bore Vert, a fret or.

Fig. 12
ESCUTCHEONS
— Timperley, knighted at the capitulation of Calais 1348, bore Gules, three escutcheons argent.

Paly. Divided into an even number of pale-like pieces. The number should be specified.

Paly-Bendy. Divided into sections formed by intersecting paly and bendy lines.

Party. A field which is divided into two by a line running in the direction of an ordinary is stated to be "party per" (or, in Scotland, "parted per") that ordinary (e.g. party per bend argent and sable). In practice the words " party" or "parted" are frequently dropped and the expression becomes "per bend", "per fess", etc.

Quarterly. Divided into four by lines in the shape of a cross (e.g. quarterly or and gules).

PARTITION LINES

The principal ornamental partition lines are eight in number. They are:

Indented	
Invected	
Engrailed	
Wavy	
Nebuly	
Embattled	
Reguly	
Dovetailed	

These lines can be either used to partition the field or to border most of the ordinaries and some of the sub-ordinaries. When an ordinary is stated to be bounded by one of these lines it implies both edges if they are both in the field (e.g. a pale is engrailed on both sides, but a chief is only engrailed on its lower edge). A bend, fess, bar and chevron are only embattled, however, on their upper edge. When both edges are affected the expression used is "embattled-counter-embattled".

Chapter V

THE COMMON CHARGES

THE common charges are all those figures which appear in arms other than the honourable ordinaries and the sub-ordinaries. Almost every conceivable object from the heraldic lion to a railway engine seems to have been incorporated in arms at one time or another. A detailed list of them would make tedious reading, even if it were possible within the compass of this work. It will be sufficient if the reader is enabled to recognise them, to describe them and to know in what fashion they should be depicted. As long as certain rules are kept, the heraldic artist has a very wide latitude, and a charge can be a thing of beauty or an artistic horror without necessarily contravening the blazon. It should be possible to draw any armorial achievement from a written blazon; and if it is not possible, the probability is that the emblems described are not truly heraldic.

The common charges fall into the following main groups:

(1) The Human Figure and Human-like Monsters
(2) Beasts and Beast-like Monsters
(3) Birds and Bird-like Monsters
(4) Fish, Reptiles and Insects
(5) Vegetation
(6) Inanimate Objects

The Monsters are an extraordinary collection of mythical creatures. Most of them seem to have owed their origin to travellers' tales and were the result of the heraldic artists' attempts to reproduce the verbal descriptions of either actual animals which the travellers had seen themselves, or else of entirely imaginary beasts whose existence had its basis in local legend.

The only charges mentioned throughout this chapter are those in common use which are drawn in a particular way in heraldry or have special heraldic names. Charges not mentioned are either easily recognisable or comparatively rare. In addition, all the common heraldic attitudes and attributes of charges are given.

THE HUMAN FIGURE AND HUMAN-LIKE MONSTERS

The human figure is not very commonly seen in arms either in whole or in part, though it is frequently used in crests and as supporters.

Arm.   An arm is generally shown with fingers clenched and as either a complete arm or else as a *cubit arm*, that is, couped or severed below the elbow. A cubit arm is generally shown erect, whilst a complete arm is *embowed* or bent at the elbow. When simply blazoned as "embowed", it is held erect and is a dexter arm unless otherwise stated. If stretched across the shield instead of upwards it is "embowed fessways". Two arms, dexter and sinister, are "counter-embowed". An arm may be *vested* or *habited*, in which case it wears a sleeve. If the cuff is of a different colour to the remainder of the sleeve, it is *cuffed*. It is frequently in armour, and the hand may be in a gauntlet.

Blackamoor.   Shown as a negro with short woolly hair.

Hand.   Generally shown couped at the wrist with fingers erect and the palm facing the spectator. It is then *apaumé*.

Head.   Shown couped at the neck and either in profile or *affronté*; that is, facing the spectator.

Merman.   A monster. The upper part of a man joined to the tail of a fish.

Mermaid.   The female of a merman. She is usually holding a mirror in one hand and a comb in the other.

Moor.   Another name for a blackamoor.

Savage.   Naked, but wreathed about the head and loins with vegetation. He is generally represented as a European with uncut brown hair and beard, and holding the bough of a tree as a club.

Saracen.   He has black hair and beard, and a twisted scarf round the temples.

Triton.   Another name for a merman.

Wild Man.   Another name for a savage.

Woman.   In heraldry she is generally young, golden-haired and beautiful (if the artist has the ability to so arrange it!).

BEASTS AND BEAST-LIKE MONSTERS

The lion is by far the most important beast in heraldry and it was, in fact, the only one used as a charge in the earliest days of armory. It was probable that originally a lion as a charge was just described as such without any proviso as to its position and that it was drawn in the manner which best suited the shape of the shield. When positions became formalised, the rampant attitude was accepted as the typical one for a lion, and a "lion rampant" was blazoned simply as a "lion". The lion was followed fairly soon by the leopard, but this animal was in practice indistinguishable from a lion, and a lion passant guardant (as in the Royal Arms of England) was held to be behaving as a leopard, and the Royal Arms were accordingly blazoned as "gules, three leopards in pale or". The only other beast used in early heraldry was the boar. Now, however, almost every known animal seems to have been used as a charge.

(a) *Heraldic Beasts*

Antelope.   The heraldic antelope is nothing like the real antelope. It has a body like a deer, a tail like a lion and a most peculiar head with straight serrated horns. The real antelope is also used in heraldry.

Ape. Usually shown as "collared and chained". The collar is placed round the animal's middle with a chain attached.

Camelopard. A giraffe. Believed by the mediaeval heralds to have been a cross between a leopard with a camel.

Cat-a-Mountain. A wild cat.

Centaur. A monster with a body of a horse and with the upper half of a man replacing the horse's head and neck. If it carries a bow and arrow it is known as a "sagittarius".

Cockatrice. Similar to a wyvern (q.v.) but with the head of a cock. It is said to have been produced from the egg laid by a nine-year-old cock on a dunghill and hatched by a toad!

Dragon. A four-legged monster, covered with scales, with a barbed tongue and tail and the wings of a bat.

Griffin. The fore part has the legs, wings and head of an eagle, whilst the remainder of the body is that of a lion. The head has ears, which is the only way it can be distinguished from an eagle's head when it is borne couped or erased. A male griffin, which is seen occasionally, has no wings, and spikes stick out from a number of points on the body. The griffin is of very early origin and representations of it are found in ancient history from the Mediterranean to Burma.

Fleece. Depicted as a dead ram suspended by a belt or surcingle round its middle.

Lion. It is usual to show the lion with his tongue and claws of a different colour to its body. If neither the lion nor the field are gules then that colour is generally used; otherwise the tongue and claws are painted azure. In the latter case the blazon would state *"armed and langued azure"*, but no mention is made if gules is used.

Lioncel. A little lion. A term sometimes used when there are a number of lions on the field.

Paschal Lamb (also referred to as the *Agnus Dei*). A lamb passant with a halo round its head and carrying a staff, surmounted by a cross, from which flies a pennon of St. George.

Pegasus. A winged horse.

Salamandar. Sometimes drawn as a wingless dragon and sometimes as a lizard. It is always surrounded by flames of fire.

Sea Monsters. There are a number of sea monsters which are generally formed by joining the fore part of an animal to the tail of a fish and giving the fore legs webbed feet. Examples are the sea lion (not to be confused with the natural animal, which also occurs in heraldry) and the sea horse. The sea dog is rather different, as it has four webbed feet instead of a fish's tail, the body is covered with scales, a fin runs down the back from head to tail, and it has the tail of a beaver.

Sphinx. A monster which has been imported by the British Army from Egypt. It has the head and breasts of a woman joined to the body of a lion.

Talbot. The original English hound.

Tyger. The heraldic tyger is quite unlike the natural beast (which also occurs as a charge). Its head is like that of the heraldic antelope, but without horns and with a mane. The remainder of the body is similar to a lion's.

Unicorn. This is probably the most familiar of the monsters from its appearance as a supporter in the Royal Arms. It has the head and mane of a horse with a single horn growing out of its forehead, a beard, the legs and feet of a deer, and the tail of a lion. It has been suggested that it has its origin in the gazelle, which is very common in Syria and which has two straight horns set closely together, so that they sometimes appear as one when the animal is seen in profile.

Wyvern.   Similar to a dragon, but with only two legs. This, as a matter of fact, is probably the original Wessex dragon, for the dragon in the Bayeux tapestry has only two legs.

(b) *Attitudes and Attributes of Heraldic Beasts*

Armed.   Refers to teeth, tusks, horns, etc. (e.g. a boar gules armed azure).

Addorsed.   Said of two animals placed back to back.

At Gaze.   The term used to describe stags and other deer when in the statant guardant position.

At Speed.   Sometimes used instead of "courant" to describe stags and other deer.

Caboshed.   Description applied to the head of such animals as stags, bulls, rams, etc., when it is drawn affronté without any portion of the neck attached.

Combatant.   Two animals rampant towards each other.

Couchant.   Lying down with head erect.

Couped.   Describes a head or limb severed from the body by a straight cut.

Courant.   Running or galloping with the legs stretched out (as in the old sporting prints).

Coward.   Having the tail passing between the hind legs. A lynx is normally shown as coward.

Dormant.   Lying down with the head resting on the fore legs.

Double-queued.   Having two tails (e.g. a lion double-queued).

Erased.   Describes a head, etc., which has been torn off the body (e.g. a boar's head erased gules). Three jagged ends are left protruding at the base of the severed portion.

Erect.   Describes a wyvern or other two-legged monster in the rampant position.

Forcene.   The term used to describe a horse in the rampant position.

Face.   The head of an animal (other than those to which the term "caboshed" is applied) affronté and without any portion of the neck attached.

Gorged.   Having a collar, coronet, etc., round the neck.

Guardant.   Said of an animal having the head alone affronté (e.g. a lion statant guardant).

Langued.   Refers to the tongue and usually used with "armed" (e.g. a lion gules armed and langued azure).

Lodged.   Used of a stag or other deer instead of couchant.

Nowed.   Tied in a knot. Generally applied to the tail.

Passant.   Walking. The animal has the off fore leg raised and the off hind leg advanced.

Queue-fourché.   A tail which forks into two (e.g. a lion rampant queue-fourché).

Rampant.   Erect with the fore legs in the air and the off hind leg raised.

Reguardant.   Having the head turned right round towards the rear (e.g. a lion rampant reguardant).

Regarding.   Two beasts passant towards each other are termed "passant regarding".

Respecting.   The term "passant respecting" is sometimes used for tame animals instead of passant regarding.

Salient.   Erect with the fore legs stretched upwards and both hind legs on the ground.

Sejant.   Sitting on the haunches with the fore legs on the ground. If the fore legs are in the rampant position the term used is *"sejant* erect". An animal seated facing the spectator with both fore legs raised is *sejant erect affronté.*

Springing.   Used to describe a stag or other deer in the salient position.

Statant.   Standing. Normally with the fore legs together and the off hind leg advanced.

Trippant.   Used instead of passant in reference to a deer.

Unguled.   Refers to hoofs (e.g. a horse arg. maned and unguled or).

BIRDS AND BIRD-LIKE MONSTERS

The eagle is the most important of the birds and occupies much the same pre-eminent position in relation to other birds as the lion does to the other beasts. There is a distinction in heraldry between birds of prey of the falcon family and other birds.

HERALDIC BIRDS

(a) *Birds of Prey*

Eagle.   An eagle is generally shown in one of three positions. These are:

> *Displayed,* i.e. affronté with wings and legs spread outwards and the tail downwards.
>
> *Rising,* i.e. standing with wings raised.
>
> *Close,* i.e. standing with wings closed.

There are many variations of these positions to which various names have been given, but it would probably be adequate to use one of these three terms and leave the detailed interpretation to the heraldic artist. If an eagle has beak and legs of a different colour to its body it is *armed and membered* of that colour. The Imperial Eagle of the Holy Roman Empire, Imperial Russia and the Austro-Hungarian Empire had two heads, one turned to the dexter and the other to the sinister. The Imperial Eagle of Napoleon had its head turned to the sinister and was always shown with the wing tips turned down, or inverted. A number of eagles displayed on a field are frequently called *eaglets.*

Falcon.   The falcon is very similar to an eagle, but is shown with a smooth head and closed beak. It is generally in the close position and is *jessed and belled*; that is, with a bell attached by a leather thong to either one or both legs.

Wings.   Wings are always presumed to be eagle's wings unless otherwise stated. A pair of wings joined at the base and displayed are stated to be *conjoined in leure* (from their similarity to the lure which was thrown into the air by a falconer to recall his hawk).

(b) *Other Birds*

Most other birds are shown as close unless they are flying, when they are *volant.* If the beak and legs are a different colour to the body, they are *beaked and membered* of that colour.

Cornish Chough.   Black with red beak and legs.

Crane.   It generally has one leg raised, holding a stone in the claw and is blazoned as a *crane in its vigilance.* This has reference to the old legend which said that if the crane fell asleep it would drop the stone and wake itself up.

Gamecock. Instead of being beaked and membered it is *armed* in reference to its beak and spurs and *combed and jelloped* about the head.

Heron. Generally holds an eel in its bill.

Martlet. An heraldic swallow, and is usually shown with no feet. It was probably originally meant to represent the swift, which is rarely seen except on the wing and was popularly supposed to be without feet.

Owl. Usually drawn with the body in the usual close position but with head the affronté.

Peacock. When affronté with tail displayed it is said to be *in its pride.*

Pelican. The heraldic pelican is really a monster, since it bears no resemblance to the actual bird. Sometimes it is very like an eagle, but it is generally drawn with a long neck and beak. It is always shown with wings raised, pecking its breast with its beak, and is said to be *vulning itself.* The pelican is usually standing in its nest with its young at its feet feeding them with drops of its blood, and is blazoned as a *pelican in her piety.* It is a favourite Christian emblem typifying Our Lord's redemption of His Children.

Phoenix. Another monster. The phoenix is shown as a demi-eagle (or the fore part of an eagle) rising with wings displayed from flames of fire.

Popinjay. A parrot.

Stork. Often holds a snake in its bill.

FISH, REPTILES AND INSECTS

Fish are said to be *naiant* in the horizontal position and *hauriant* in the vertical. Serpents are generally *nowed*, or tied in a knot.

Bee. The most common of insects and very popular in civic arms to represent industry. A gold bee was adopted as a badge by Napoleon and was used by him to replace the fleur-de-lis.

Dolphin. Really a monster, as it is most unlike the fish of this name. It is shown curved and is blazoned *embowed.* When "proper" it has green scales and red fins.

Pike. Known as a *luce* in England and a *ged* in Scotland.

Salmon. Drawn with a square-ended tail.

VEGETATION

All kinds of vegetation are used as heraldic charges, particularly trees, flower and leaves.

Cinquefoil. A conventional five-petalled clover leaf, without a stalk. Sometimes called a *fraise*, or strawberry leaf (as in the arms of Fraser), or a *primrose* (as in the arms of Primrose). It is sometimes found pierced in the centre.

Eradicated. Pulled up by the roots. Said of a tree when it is shown with roots attached.

Garb. A sheaf of corn. It is one of the oldest charges in heraldry.

Quatrefoil. A conventional four-petalled clover leaf without a stalk.

Rose. The heraldic rose is a conventionalised form of the wild rose. It is generally blazoned as *barbed and seeded*, with reference to the thorns which appear between the petals and the seeds in the middle of the flower (e.g. a rose gules, barbed vert, seeded or). If it has a stalk with leaves on it it is *slipped and leaved.* Roses are, of course, well-known badges of England and they will be discussed in greater detail in the chapter on badges.

Slipped. Having a stalk. Used in reference to a leaf or flower.

Stock. A tree stump. It is frequently seen couped and eradicated. That is, cut short by the felling of a tree and pulled up by the roots.

Tree. If the type of tree is not specified it is drawn as an oak tree. The fruit and leaves are drawn very large, in order that the type of tree may be easily recognisable.

Trefoil. A conventional three-petalled clover leaf and always drawn slipped. In Irish arms, particularly, it is now generally drawn very much more like the natural shamrock.

INANIMATE OBJECTS

A vast number of charges are included under the above heading and new ones are being constantly added. Industry has already been responsible for shuttles, cogwheels, aircraft propellers, shovels, corded bales, paddle-steamers, locomotives and many others. Some of these modern charges are unhappy choices; others have a simple and symbolic form in the true heraldic tradition. Most inanimate charges can be identified without difficulty, but some of the older ones are not so obvious or have special heraldic names.

Caltrap. A small metal object of four sharp points thrown on the ground as a defence against cavalry (the mediaeval anti-tank mine).

Castle. Generally shown as two towers with a connecting embattled wall with a doorway. If there is a third tower in the middle of the castle wall it is called a *castle triple towered.*

Chess Rook. It has the base of a piece used for the game, but the top is splayed out into two tongues.

Clarion. A J-shaped figure with an organ-pipe top. Nobody knows what it is, though it is most commonly supposed to be a musical instrument.

Crescent. A crescent of the moon with the horns turned upwards. If the horns are turned to the dexter it is an *increscent* and if to the sinister a *decrescent.*

Escallop. The pilgrim's shell. It was widely adopted as a charge at the time of the Crusades and was the badge of pilgrims going to the Holy Land.

Escarbuncle. An ornamental boss with eight sceptres radiating from it and terminating in fluers-de-lis. It has its origin in an identical method of strengthening the shield with a metal boss and decorative iron bands.

Estoile. A star with long wavy rays.

Lymphad. An ancient ship with one mast.

Maunch. A mediaeval lady's sleeve with a long hanging cuff.

Millrind. Sometimes called a fer de *moline.* It is the iron from the centre of a mill-stone. It is rather remarkable that the same design has been used through the centuries until the present day.

Mullet. A star with short straight points. Unless otherwise stated there are five of them. Its name really means a spur rowel and not a star. In Scotland, however, a mullet is only so called if it is pierced; and if it is not pierced it is called a star.

Pheon. A broad arrow head of which the inside edge of the barb is engrailed.

Portcullis. Drawn as a kind of barred frame with a chain hanging down from each side of the top.

Seax. A scimitar with a curved notch at the back of the blade.

Sun in splendour. When so blazoned, the sun generally has a human face on its surface and it has alternate straight and wavy rays projecting from the circumference. The straight rays represent light and the wavy ones heat.

Tower. A single tower with a doorway. If it has three small towers on top of it, it is called a *tower triple towered.*

Water Bouget. A mediaeval vessel for carrying water consisting of two leather pouches suspended from a yoke.

SEMÉ

The term "semé" is used when the field is strewn with small charges some of which may be defaced by the edge of the field (e.g. semé of torteaux). In the case of some charges certain special names are generally used. These are:

> Bezante (Semé of bezants)
> Billety   (Semé of billets)
> Crusilly (Semé of crosslets)
> Flory, or Semé-de-lis (Semé of fleurs-de-lis)
> Platé   (Semé of plates)

A field is sometimes covered with pear-shaped drops of liquid called "gouttes". The word "gutté" is used to describe such a field, followed by the type of drops. Thus:

> Gutté d'or   (gold drops)
> Gutté d'eau   (silver drops)
> Gutté de sang (red drops)
> Gutté de larmes (blue drops)
> Gutté d'huile (green drops)
> Gutté de poix (black drops)

Chapter VI

BLAZONING COUNTERCHANGING AND MARSHALLING

BLAZON

A "BLAZON" is a verbal description of arms. "To blazon" is to give that description, and it should not be confused with "to emblazon", which means to depict arms in colour.

The heraldic language used to describe an achievement of arms sometimes strikes the uninitiated as rather archaic and an unnecessary added complication to the mastery of heraldry. It is, however, clear and concise, and is generally the shortest possible method of giving an accurate description of arms.

THE FIELD

Every blazon starts with a description of the field. If the field is merely partitioned without any charges it might be, for instance,

Per pale indented argent and gules.

It will be noted that the first thing mentioned is the method of partition, then any special partition line and finally the tinctures. The tincture of the senior part of the shield (in this case, of course, the dexter) is mentioned first. In the case of "quarterly" the first and fourth quarters (that is, those in the dexter chief and sinister base) are described first, followed by the second and third; thus,

Quarterly argent and gules.

Similarly, in a multi-partitioned field the partition nearest to the dexter chief is the first mentioned; e.g.

Chequy argent and gules.

Whilst it is not necessary for a partitioned field to be parted of a metal and a colour, it is comparatively rarely that two metals or two colours are found.

THE PRINCIPAL CHARGE

The next thing described is the principal charge. No charge normally takes precedence of a bend, fess, pale, pile, chevron, cross or saltire, except one of themselves, when positioning on the field will normally decide the priority. A field with one of these charges would be blazoned

> *Azure, a bend engrailed or.*

Punctuation is kept to a minimum, and it is normal to restrict commas to one after each tincture.

SECONDARY CHARGES

After the principal charge, the secondary charge or charges are described; e.g.

> *Argent, a chevron between three stags statant sable.*

Here the chevron is the principal charge and the stags are secondary. As both chevron and stags are black, the word "sable" is placed only at the end of the blazon.

The stags might be additionally described as "two and one", to indicate two in chief and one in base, but where a chevron lies between three charges it is always understood that this is how they are disposed unless otherwise stated.

CHARGES ON AN ORDINARY

Instead of being between charges, an ordinary might be charged with them; thus,

> *Vert, on a fess argent, three mullets of the field.*

The mullets are vert, but repetitions in a blazon are avoided if possible. The expressions used are "of the field", or, alternatively, "of the first", 'of the second", etc., according to the order in which the colour referred to has appeared.

Charges on an ordinary are mentioned after secondary charges on the field; e.g.

> *Gules, on a chevron between three falcons close argent, as many pellets.*

The words "as many" are used here to avoid a repetition of "three".

ORDINARIES MENTIONED AT THE END OF THE BLAZON

The chief, canton, flaunch and bordure together with any charges which they bear are generally mentioned after the remainder of the shield has been blazoned; e.g.

> *Argent, on a chevron engrailed sable, between three griffin's heads erased gules, as many annulets or; a chief of the second charged with a lion passant reguardant gold.*

The use of the word "gold" is customary in a blazon when mention of this metal is made for the second time. A semi-colon is an appropriate punctuation before describing the chief and its charges.

AN ORDINARY OVERALL

If an ordinary surmounts everything else on the field, then the normal order of precedence is waived and the ordinary is stated to be "overall", and will be mentioned at the end of the blazon; e.g.

Ermine, a lion rampant vert, overall a bendlet or.

SEMÉ

Objects which are "semé" are considered to be part of the field, and are therefore mentioned before any other charge.

Arg., billety az., a lion rampant gu., armed and langued of the second.

The order of blazoning is therefore:

(1) The field
(2) Anything semé
(3) The principal charge
(4) The secondary charges
(5) Any charges borne by the principal charge
(6) Any chief, canton, flaunch or bordure
(7) Any charges borne by the above
(8) Any ordinary placed overall

POSITION OF COMMON CHARGES

If the positioning of common charges is not obvious, it must be stated; e.g.

Arg., a chevron between four martlets, three in chief and one in base gu.

DIRECTION OF CHARGES

In the case of swords and similar charges which might point either way, the direction must be specified; e.g.

Gu., three swords fesswise in pale, points to the dexter ppr., hilted or.

The following example shows a more complicated arrangement of swords:

Gu., three swords bendwise in pale arg., the hilts to the chief or; on a chief az., two fleurs-de-lis gold.

Here the three swords are each bendwise, one below and parallel to the other.

A good blazon sounds right. It avoids repetitions, is brief, has no redundant words and gives an accurate description of an armorial achievement. But the object of a blazon is to give an accurate description, and in some really complicated arms it may be impossible to do this without unpleasant-sounding repetitions. In that case euphony must give way to tautology. If faced with a difficult coat of arms, the best way of tackling it is to write down the description without bothering about the phraseology and then to try and tidy it up into a neat blazon by arranging the charges in their correct order, eliminating redundant words and replacing repetitions.

TRICK

There is another method of describing arms which is known as a "trick". This is an outline drawing of arms with the tinctures indicated by abbreviations. Charges which recur twice or more are only drawn once. The figure 1 is placed beside the charge shown and the figures 2, 3, etc., are inserted in the other parts of the shield where the same charge would appear. The ordinary heraldic abbreviations may be used for the tinctures, but the following are more usual; "A" for argent, "O" for or, "B" for azure, "G" for gules, "S" for sable, "Vt" for vert and "Purp" for purpure.

COUNTERCHANGING

When a shield is divided into parts of one metal and one colour and the charges so arranged that the metal always appears on the colour and vice versa, the word "counterchanged" is used to shorten the blazon; e.g.

(a) *Quarterly, arg. and gu., a cross counterchanged.*
In this example each limb of the cross is divided lengthways and tinctured according to the part of the field on which it lies.

(b) *Per pale or and az., a chevron between three annulets all counterchanged.*
In this case the chevron and the annulet in base are each half azure and half or. The annulet in dexter chief is azure and that in sinister chief, or.

(c) *Per fess or and vert, a pale counterchanged.*
This is quite difficult to recognise as a counterchange because it divides the shield into six equal divisions.

To complete this section a curious coat of arms is shown. It belonged to Renaud de Pressigny, Marshal of France in 1270. J. Woodward states that the coat was considered so difficult to describe clearly and succinctly as to be a test of a man's knowledge of French blazon. Its description is not a bad test of a mastery of English blazon, and the reader is invited to try. A suggested solution will be found at the end of this chapter.

MARSHALLING

The marshalling together of two or more shields of arms probably originated when the representation of two houses devolved on one man and he inherited the arms of both. The earliest form of marshalling is found on old seals, where two or more shields are placed together in an artistic arrangement. One of the shields is generally recognisable as the most important. The first attempt to combine different arms on one shield resulted in the "composed" coat, in which charges were taken from the various arms to form one composite coat. This was a popular method in the fourteenth century.

The arms of husband and wife were probably first marshalled by placing them side by side. This disposition of the shields was known as "accolée" and is still used where, for instance, the husband's shield is encircled by the collar or circlet of an order.

Modern marshalling is used to denote (1) sovereignty and dominion, as in the British Royal Arms; (2) alliance, as in the joint achievement of a husband and wife or the temporary union of personal arms with arms of office; (3) descent, where two or more coats of arms are inherited through the marriage into a family of heraldic heiresses; (4) pretension, as when a man marries an heraldic heiress and "pretends" to the representation of her family.

DIMIDIATION AND IMPALEMENT

In the first union of a husband's and wife's arms on one shield they were so drawn that the husband's arms appeared to overlap those of the wife, leaving only half the latter showing. (There is at least one thirteenth-century example of the arms as borne by a wife being placed on the dexter side overlapping those of her husband on the sinister, i.e. Devorgilla, daughter of Alan of Galloway and wife of John Balliol.)

By the fourteenth century the practice of "dimidiation" was used fairly extensively in England to marshal the arms of husband and wife. It was merely a development of the overlapping method by which both arms were cut in half down the palar line and the dexter half of the husband's joined to the sinister half of the wife's. It was an unsatisfactory system, and although it lingered to the end of the sixteenth century it was already being replaced by "impalement" towards the end of the fourteenth. The arms of the Cinque Ports provide an example of the extraordinary results which were sometimes produced by dimidiation. The foreparts of the three lions passant guardant of England are joined to the stern ends of three ships.

In impalement both coats of arms are placed side by side on the shield complete, and this is the system used at present both for the arms of husband and wife and to marshal the official and personal arms of bishops, officers of arms, etc. An interesting example of dimidiation still lingers. When one of the impaled coats has a bordure it is not continued down the centre of the shield but stops short top and bottom at the palar line. This ruling also applies to the tressure.

QUARTERING

Quartering is probably an older system of marshalling than either dimidiation or impalement, and was adopted as an alternative to the composed coat as a method of marshalling arms of lordships. The shield is divided into at least four sections by fesswise and palewise partition lines, and a complete coat of arms is displayed in each section. Although the terms "quartering", "quarters" and "quarterly" are used, the number of sections is not limited to four in English armory; in fact it is unlimited, but there is generally an even number. In a quartered coat in English heraldry the principal arms always appear in the dexter chief quarter, and, if only two or if an indivisible number (5, 7, 11, etc.) of coats of arms are being quartered, they are repeated in the last quarter; that is, in the sinister base. In Scotland there is no definite rule as regards the order in which arms shall be marshalled, but it is stated in each matriculation. The arms in a shield with multiple quarterings may be arranged in the number of rows which best suits the shape of the shield and the charges in the various arms.

Another method of marshalling quarterings is known as "quarterly quartered" or "grand quartering". The number of quarters in the shield are restricted to four, but each of these quarters may again be quartered. Each of the small quarters are called "quarters", whilst the large quarters are "grand quarters". This is the system which is normally used in Scotland. It was the Scottish practice in the seventeenth century to limit the number of arms displayed to six. That is now often exceeded, but the system of quarterly quartering places practical limits on the number of arms which may be marshalled together. The Chiefs of the House of Atholl are entitled to upwards of a thousand quarterings, but there is no record of their ever having tried to show them on one shield.

The Royal Arms, which constitute a simple quartered coat, are

PLATE 8

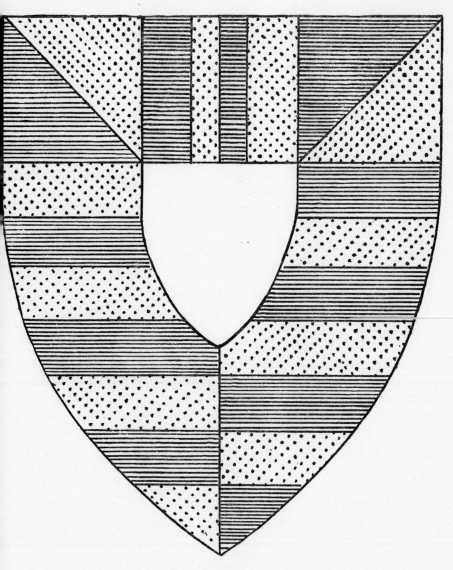

ARMS OF RENAUD DE PRESSIGNY, MARSHAL OF FRANCE

blazoned as follows ("1st" is the dexter chief, "2nd" the sinister chief, "3rd" the dexter base and "4th" the sinister base):

> *Quarterly, 1st and 4th, Gu., three lions passant guardant in pale or (England): 2nd, Or, a lion rampant gu., armed and langued az., within a tressure flory-counter-flory of the second (Scotland): 3rd, Az., a harp or, stringed arg. (Ireland).*

If there were six quarters the blazon would have started "Quarterly of six". In this case the numbers would run in order, the 6th quarter being the sinister base.

The arms of the Stuarts as Kings of England provide an example of a quarterly quartered shield:

> *Quarterly 1st and 4th grand quarters, quarterly i and iv, Az., three fleurs-de-lis or (France); ii and iii, Gu., three lions passant guardant in pale or (England): 2nd grand quarter, Or, a lion rampant gu., armed and langued az., within a tressure flory-counter-flory of the second (Scotland): 3rd grand quarter, Az., a harp or stringed arg. (Ireland).*

THE INESCUTCHEON

In the centre of the shield is sometimes placed a smaller shield of arms, which debruises the arms borne on the former. It may, in Scottish practice, bear the paternal arms, feudal arms or arms of alliance. In English heraldry it has been used since the sixteenth century to denote arms of alliance, when the wife is an heraldic heiress, and is known as an "inescutcheon of pretence".

The rules regarding the inheritance of arms and the order in which they are placed on the shield will be dealt with in the next chapter.

PUZZLE SOLUTION

The suggested solution for the blazon of the de Pressigny arms (see Plate 8) is:

> *Per pale or and az., three bars counterchanged; on a chief parted and tinctured as the field two pallets between as many gyrons all counterchanged; an inescutcheon arg.*

Chapter VII

INHERITANCE OF ARMS

THIS chapter deals with the correct method of bearing personal arms. That is, how the arms to which a person is entitled are marshalled, and how arms of different members of the same family are distinguished one from the other. The latter will be dealt with first.

CADENCY AND DIFFERENCING

The principle that no two men should bear precisely the same arms was generally accepted by the fourteenth century, and it was the practice for cadet lines, that is the younger sons of a family and their descendants, to use the arms of the head of the house with some conspicuous mark of difference. The choice of these marks was, at that time, left to the persons concerned. The earliest mark of cadency in general use appears to have been the label, which probably dates from the first half of the thirteenth century. Originally it merely showed that the bearer of the arms was not the head of the house. It was followed by the bordure, which was used for the same purpose and possibly also to indicate bastardy. Gradually many methods of differencing arms were adopted in order to ensure that all members of the same house should have their own distinctive coats. These methods included changing the tinctures, adding charges, altering the position of charges, substituting charges, adding ordinaries, changing partition lines and several others. At the end of the sixteenth century a system of cadency marks was introduced which eventually became standardised in English armory. In this system the label was reserved for an eldest son. Marks were allotted to the other sons as follows: for the second, a crescent; for the third, a mullet; for the fourth, a martlet; for the fifth, an annulet; for the sixth, a fleur-de-lis; for the seventh, a rose; for the eighth, a cross moline; for the ninth, a double quatrefoil.

The old writers have provided meanings for these different symbols. The label of three points was to signify that the eldest son was the third in precedence, following his father and mother. His own eldest son was allotted a label of five points. The second son's crescent showed that he should increase the family by adding to its estate and repute. The mullet, or spur rowel, of the third son was to incite him to chivalry (presumably a traditionally boorish individual!). The fourth son's martlet indicated that he would inherit little land to rest upon and would have to rely on the wings of his own endeavours. The annulet, as a symbol of great actions, was a similar encouragement to the fifth son. The fleur-de-lis was allotted to the sixth son "to put him in mind of his Country and his Prince". The seventh had a rose in order that he should try and flourish like it. The eighth son's cross moline, known as an "anchoring cross", was to remind him "to grip when he can fasten, seeing he has nothing else to which he may trust". The double quatrefoil of the ninth carried the unkind reminder that there were eight brothers between him and the succession! These cadency marks were originally intended as purely temporary distinctions to be used by sons during the life of their father or until they married and started houses of their own, when they would be granted a properly differenced coat. The differencing of the arms of cadet lines has remained the practice in Scottish armory until the present day, but in England the cadency marks gradually took the place of differencing and became the only means of distinguishing between the arms of different houses of the same family.

The cadency mark is usually placed in the middle chief point, in the case of a single coat. A quartered shield is normally differenced by placing the mark on the fess point or, if multiple quartering makes this impossible without differencing only one coat, by putting it on a partition line as near to the fess point as possible. Any tinctures may be used for cadency marks except that the label may not be white—which is reserved for labels of the Royal Family. Authorities differ as to whether the tincture rule applies to a cadency mark or not. The present tendency is to say that it does not, and a colour is sometimes placed on a colour, or a metal on a metal, to indicate that the object is a cadency mark and not a charge.

So far this system of cadency is simple. It is when it is carried a stage further to the grandsons of the original head of the house that difficulties arise. If a man's cadency mark is a crescent, all his sons will assume that crescent, but the eldest son will charge the crescent with a label, the second will charge it with another crescent, the third son with a mullet, and so on. If now the original head of the house dies, his eldest son will succeed him and will discard his label. The eldest son of the new head of the house will exchange his five-point label for one with three points, the second son will cease to bear a label charged with a crescent and will bear a crescent alone, and any other brothers will alter their marks similarly. But the second son of the new head of the house will be bearing the same cadency mark as his uncle, who is the second son of the original head. The second son of a second son, whose father is still alive and was also a second son, would bear, in theory, a crescent charged with another crescent which in turn is charged with a third crescent. It will be readily appreciated, too, that in the case of a large

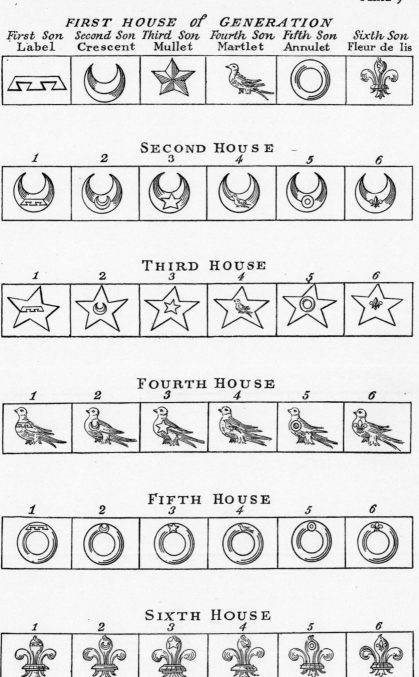

ENGLISH CADENCY MARKS

family with many branches there may be two or more cousins bearing the same cadency mark.

The operation of this system in a mythical family with several branches is shown in the diagram. It will be noted that, whilst one particular cadency mark is liable to become permanent in one cadet line of a family, in other instances these marks are continually changing as death alters heraldic relationships. In practice, the system can be made to work rather better than at first appears. If a member of a cadet line marries an heraldic heiress and quarters her family arms, he removes his cadency mark. The quartered coat will then be differenced as a whole by his descendants as if he had obtained an entirely fresh grant of arms. The use of these cadency marks is not compulsory, and the individual may choose either not to bear one at all or merely to display the one cadency mark of his line without any other charged upon it. Some authorities hold, with some reason, however, that it is improper for any cadet to display the undifferenced arms of the head of the house. If an exemplification of arms (on the creation of a peerage, for instance) should carry a cadency mark, then in this case it does become obligatory to display it in future. In theory, crests should be differenced as well as shields. In practice, if cadency marks are used, they are generally only single ones owing to the practical difficulties of charging such a necessarily small charge with another one.

As has already been said, the old method of differencing arms remained the practice in Scotland. The cadency marks of English armory have been used to a certain extent in Scotland in the past and even appear as hereditary figures in some Scottish arms, but they have never been generally adopted. During their father's lifetime the eldest son bears his father's arms debruised by a label, but the younger sons have no arms until they have been assigned a differenced shield. The methods of differencing in Scotland at the beginning of the present century were as follows:

(1) Change of the tinctures of the charges
(2) Addition of new charges; particularly the bordure and chevron
(3) Alteration of boundary lines of ordinaries, etc.
(4) Change of the form or attitude of charges
(5) Alteration of the number of charges
(6) Alteration of the position of the charges on the field
(7) Substitution of one charge by another

The late Mr. Stodart, who was Lyon Clerk Depute (1864-86), devised a method of differencing arms which is now generally used for

68

PLATE 10

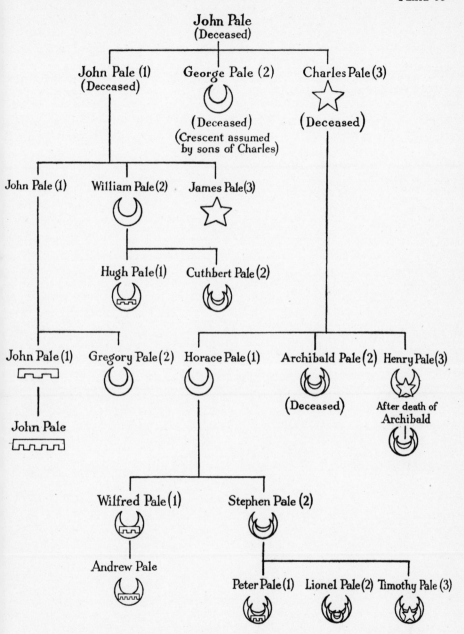

THE PRACTICAL USE AND DUPLICATION OF CADENCY MARKS IN AN IMAGINARY
FAMILY

new matriculations by cadets (see Plate 11). Differencing in Scotland is compulsory. The undifferenced coat belongs exclusively to the head of the family, and cadets are not entitled to use arms until they "matriculate" their ancestors' arms in their own names. Lyon King of Arms assigns the difference he considers suitable to the paternal coat and the differenced arms are matriculated in the Lyon Register in the name of the petitioner.

INHERITED ARMS

The inheritance of arms belonging to other families is largely accidental. The rule is that a wife may not pass on her arms to her children unless she is an heraldic heiress or co-heiress and her husband is armigerous. Arms always descend through the male line if possible, but if there are no male descendants of a line, or if they die without leaving children then the arms may descend through the female line. A woman is an heraldic heiress if she is an only child, or a co-heiress if she has one or more sisters. She may become an heiress after her death through her brothers dying without leaving any children; in which case her children inherit her arms. It will be seen, therefore, that whilst one family may possess the same single coat for hundreds of years, another family possessing arms of comparatively recent grant may amass a large number of quarterings through the marriage into the family of two or three heiresses whose own coats are already quartered. As has already been said, quartering was originally used to denote union of lordships. It was only when arms ceased to be used practically in the field that the present system arose of quartering arms which carry no estate or position with them.

When a man marries a wife of an armigerous family who is not an heiress, he may impale her arms with his own, but only her pronominal (single paternal) coat. If she should subsequently become an heiress, then he places her arms, with any quarterings to which she is entitled, on an inescutcheon of pretence on his own shield (see Plate 12). His children now may quarter his two coats. If neither of them are already quartered, the procedure is simple. The father's arms are placed in the first and fourth quarters, and the mother's in the second and third. If, now, a son of the family were to marry another heiress with a single coat, his children would place it in the third quarter, leaving the arms of the first heiress in the second quarter. If yet another heiress married into the family her children would place her arms in the fourth quarter, and the original paternal coat would appear in the first quarter only.

In English armory the children of a fourth heiress could divide the shield into six quarters. It would then consist of 1st (dexter chief), pro-

PLATE 11

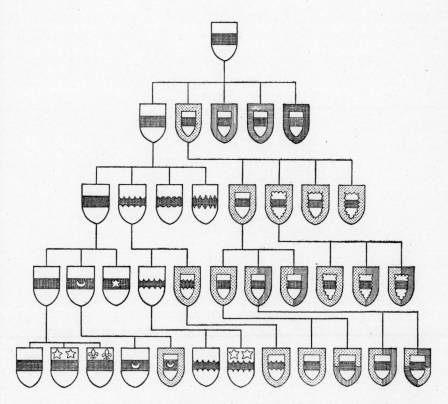

THE CADENCY DIFFERENCING SCHEME DEVISED BY MR. STODART AND USED IN THE
COURT OF THE LORD LYON

nominal arms; 2nd (middle chief), first heiress; 3rd (sinister chief), second heiress; 4th (dexter base), third heiress; 5th (middle base), fourth heiress; 6th (sinister base), pronominal arms. We will presume, now, that the only child of this last marriage is a daughter and that she marries a man who has a simple quartered coat, with his father's arms in the first and fourth quarters and his mother's in the second and third. The children will give their father's arms precedence. In the first quarter will be their paternal grandfather's arms and in the second their paternal grandmother's. Then follow their mother's arms, which will be placed in the order in which we have already dealt with them, that is, in the third quarter, the pronominal coat; in the fourth, those of the first heiress; in the fifth, the second heiress; in the sixth, the third heiress; in the seventh, the fourth heiress. An eighth quarter will obviously be required, and in this the father's paternal coat will be repeated. These quarters would probably be arranged in two rows of four.

The procedure for working out the quarterings to which anyone is entitled, therefore, and the order in which they are marshalled, is as follows. Put the paternal coat down first. Then follow the male line of the family back to the first heiress. Her arms will come next. If they are quartered, her male line will have to be traced in the same way for heiresses. When all her quarterings have been placed in the right order, proceed to the next heiress and deal with her arms, and so on till all the quarterings are in the correct sequence. It is then merely a matter of marshalling the quarterings in the most suitable way on the shield.

There is no compulsion to bear quarterings at all; alternatively, it is permissible to select the one which the bearer of the arms wishes to display on his shield. But if any of the quartered arms of any heraldic heiress are selected for quartering, her pronominal cost must be included; and, similarly, if a particular quartering came into her family through a line of heiresses, every coat of arms in the male line which bought that quartering in must be included. If the arms of an eminent family have been acquired, therefore, by a series of marriages, it is not permissible to show them in a simple quartering with the pronominal arms.

The Scottish system is very different. As in cadency differencing, it is a development of the mediaeval practice which English armory grew away from. On marriage, a wife's arms, including any quarterings, are impaled. It is unusual in Scottish heraldry to quarter arms unless estates or some position or representation follow the marriage. Nor does a husband normally place his wife's arms upon an inescutcheon of pretence if she is an heiress. He merely impales them, unless she is a peeress in her own right. Quarterings, too, are not officially recognised without a

PLATE 12

John Son of William ⸗ Ann Daur. & Heir of
Married 6 June 1700   George Died 4 May
died 6 Aug. 1720 Æ. 60   1726 Æ: 56

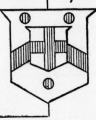

Thomas Son of John ⸗ Mary Daur. & Heir of
Married 16 June 1727   Samuel died 17 Mar
Ob⁵ 8 Feb⁹ 1767 Æ 58   1767 aged 67

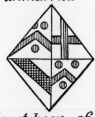

George Son of Thomas   Sarah Daur. of Tho⁵
born 10 Nov 1766 living   born 10 Nov 1751
unmarried   unmarried

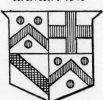

The right of Quartering by Escutcheon of
Pretence. Shews that George & his Sister Sarah
are entitled to Quarter the Arms of their Mother
& Grandmother. being Heirs Female

rematriculation of the arms, and, once matriculated, are normally indivisible. It does not necessarily follow that the pronominal coat occupies the first quarter. In the case of a cadet line a son may consider that his representation of his mother's house is the more important in view of some distinction or fief which he acquires. The system of grand quartering follows from the indivisible coat; for if inherited quartered arms cannot be broken up, they must be placed together in one of the quarters of the shield. As was pointed out in the last chapter, the Scottish method limits the number of arms which can be borne on one shield to four quartered coats or a maximum of sixteen quarterings. Many Scottish quarterings represent estates, hereditable offices, etc. Such arms are sometimes shown on an inescutcheon. The paternal arms themselves are occasionally shown on an inescutcheon. A non-armigerous husband may use his wife's arms, if she is an heiress, by the "courtesy of Scotland". But he must adopt her name as well. Though some authorities hold that a Scottish quartered coat inherited by an English family may be broken up, it is more normal, and certainly better practice, to retain it in its quartered form in a grand quarter.

THE BEARING OF ARMS BY A LADY

An unmarried lady bears her father's arms undifferenced except for any difference which her father may use. She may, of course, quarter any arms which she inherits from her mother. By a rule which dates from 1561 her arms are always displayed on a lozenge instead of a shield, and they are usually surmounted by a "true lover's knot" of blue ribbon (in Scotland the ribbon is usually the livery colours of the arms), though this is purely ornamental and not officially part of the achievement. A lady may not use crest, helm or mantling. (In Scotland she may use a crest as a badge, and a duchess may use crest and motto.) Whilst the rules for a spinster are clear, there is no ruling in English armory as to how a married lady should display her arms.

On marriage, her husband impales her arms with his own (or places them on an inescutcheon if she is an heiress), but during the period when the laws and customs of heraldry were evolving a married woman had practically no legal status. The concensus of opinion seems to be that she should not bear her own arms alone, but should show her husband's impaled with them to show she is married, and on a shield to show he is alive. This would follow Scottish practice. Fox-Davies suggests that the shield should be surmounted by a true lover's knot to show that the bearer of the shield is a lady. This seems a sound solution, for in mediaeval times, though they did not bear a shield, ladies *wore* their arms impaled with their husbands, as can be seen on memorial brasses and effigies.

A widow bears the arms of her late husband on her lozenge, with her own arms impaled, or on an escutcheon of pretence if she is an heiress. Until recently there was no regulation in England governing the bearing of arms by a lady whose marriage had been dissolved by the Civil Authority; but the College of Arms have now ruled that she should revert to the arms she bore before her marriage, charged with a mascle for difference. The children of the marriage bears their arms in the normal way. The Scottish ruling is that a lady who is an innocent party bears arms as if she were a widow. But that if she is the guilty party she reverts to her premarital maiden lozenge.

If a husband is entitled to display the insignia of an order he must show two shields; the dexter bearing his own arms and displaying the insignia of the order, and the sinister charged with his own and his wife's arms impaled. If his degree in his order entitles him to surround his shield with a circlet, he may place a decorative wreath round the sinister shield to balance the achievement. Supporters would be placed outside the two shields.

If a gentleman marries a peeress in her own right he places her arms upon an inescutcheon of pretence ensigned with her coronet. He cannot, however, use her supporters, and consequently his wife's arms are repeated on the sinister side of his own achievement on a lozenge with her coronet and supporters.

If, however, the lady is a peeress in her own right by creation, he cannot place her arms upon an inescutcheon, because she is not an heiress. The two achievements are then merely shown side by side.

Chapter VIII

THE ACCESSORIES

THE chief accessories of the shield comprise the crest, helm, wreath, crest coronet, chapeau, mantling, supporters, compartment and motto. Other accessories, such as crowns, coronets, badges and the insignia of orders will be dealt with in later chapters.

THE CREST

There is a considerable measure of disagreement amongst heraldic authorities as to the origin and use of crests. As worn on the helmet, the crest was a large device, generally modelled in cuirbouilli, or in cloth over a wood or wire framework with a stuffing inside. It was a top-heavy addition to the helm and, for that reason, it is unlikely that a crest of this nature was worn in battle, and its combat use was almost certainly restricted to the tournament. The three folios of Scottish Arms included in the fourteenth-century Armorial de Gelre give a good idea of the size and appearance of these crests. The earliest known form of crest is the lion painted on the headdress of Geoffrey, Count of Anjou, as depicted in his armorial slab of 1150; and in the second half of the twelfth century similar charges appear on helmets. From the end of the twelfth century until the beginning of the fourteenth, a fan-shaped sheet of metal was frequently worn on top and from front to rear of the helmet. Fox-Davies suggested that this was to afford greater protection from a downward blow on the helm. These fans lent themselves to decoration and were often painted with a device which was in most cases adapted from one of the charges on the shield. The crest which was assumed by the City of London is an example. On the seal of 1539 this appears on top of the helm as a fan charged with the red cross from the arms, and is so shown in Guillim's *Display of Heraldry*. In the course of time the fan has become a dragon's wing. Fox-Davies is of the opinion that the next stage of crest development was the cutting of the metal fan into the shape of the device painted on it, and instances some German crests which have the back adorned with a fan. Another instance can be found in the Scottish folios of the Armorial de Gelre. Light crests of this kind and plumes of feathers could, of course, have been borne in battle. Wings, which are often seen in crests, are probably a development of the fan. Crests modelled "in the round" first began to appear in the thirteenth century, and were possibly originally a "de luxe" edition of the fan crest for ceremonial and tournament wear. Mathieu de Martmorency, Constable of France in 1224, appears to have started a new fashion in crests when he placed a peacock's head and neck on his helm; a device which did not appear on his shield.

Many heraldic writers have asserted that the crest was awarded as an additional privilege, but there appears to be no proof to support this. Crests were frequently changed in mediaeval times and were originally so little connected with their owners' arms that they were not added to the achievement as displayed on seals until the end of the thirteenth or the beginning of the fourteenth century. From about 1315 onwards they were quite common in England, but in Scotland they were not shown in achievements until 1334. If crests were a special honour, it is unlikely that, human nature being what it is, they would have been omitted from the achievement. It is far more likely that crests were always assumed, except in the case of a few special grants, and that they were regarded neither as hereditary nor permanent. King Edward III sometimes used an eagle as a crest, and in 1333 he granted it to William Montacute, Earl of Salisbury, and, by a subsequent concession, made it hereditary. J. H. Stevenson, in his outstanding work *Heraldry in Scotland*, states that the crest was a badge of the wearer which he selected to place on top of his helmet. Very often he chose as a badge one of the charges from his shield of arms. The fact that many old English families never assumed a crest is no argument in favour of their being a special honour, for a country family which never took part in a tournament and never attended ceremonies would have no occasion to wear a crest.

The inclusion of crests with grants of arms began to be a normal practice about the end of the sixteenth century. At that time and in the seventeenth century there are many instances of grants of crests to ancient arms, though it is very likely that in the majority of cases these were recordings of crests which had already been assumed. In the last two hundred, and very likely three hundred, years no grant of arms to a non-armigerous man has ever been made without a crest. On the other hand there appears to be evidence that the right to assume a crest existed in England, though not in Scotland, up till the end of the eighteenth century. The Rev. James Dallaway, in his *Inquiries into the Origin and Progress of Heraldry in England*, is of the opinion as late as 1793 that "crests are not held to be absolutely hereditable but may be assumed". T. E. Banks, in his *Additions* to Sir William Dugdale's *Antient Usage*, published in 1812, says of the crest, "which, making no part of the arms, has generally been considered as assumable and changeable at the will of the bearer;—and even in the most rigid times heralds or Kings of arms had an authority to grant them without the priority or approbation

PLATE 13

FIRST FOLIO OF SCOTTISH ARMS IN THE ARMORIAL DE GELRE (Fourteenth Century)

EARL OF MONTEITH—EARL OF CARRICK—EARL OF FIFE

KING ROBERT II

EARL OF STRATHERN—EARL OF DOUGLAS—EARL OF MARCH

EARL OF MAR—KING OF MAN—EARL OF MORAY—EARL OF LENNOX—EARL OF ANNANDALE.

gꝛ de
ros

gꝛ de
rar
ric

gꝛ
de
biue

die co
nic hā
korlāt

gꝛ a

ſira
ale

gꝛ
a
douglas

gꝛ
de
maerche

gꝛ
de mar

kín
caman

gꝛ
de morref

gꝛ
a
teue
lenos

an ā derdeel

of the marshal. When *purchasing grants* of arms became fashionable a crest was generally thrown into the bargain." Assumption of a crest, however, obviously conferred no right of exclusive possession. Referring to the granting of crests, J. H. Stevenson, one of the most eminent of Scottish authorities, holds that, within limits, heraldic authorities are continually acting on the principle that no individual property on crests exists.

In mentioning Scottish and Irish families that bear the same crests he expresses the opinion that the practice can only be explained by regarding the crest as a kind of family totem which may be given to anyone who is a member of the same family or who even has the same surname, in the same way that a tartan may be worn by anybody who is a member of the clan. This excellent practice has not been followed, at any rate for very many years, in English armory, with the result that many ugly effects have been produced in order to achieve distinction between crests.

Since the crest was essentially meant to be borne on the helm, it is unfortunate that many crests have been granted, particularly in the mid-nineteenth century (but including at least one very recent example), which could never have been so worn. A crest should be capable of being modelled, should bear inspection from any angle and should be easily attachable to a helm. Over the last fifty years there has, in general, been a return to simplicity and a high standard of design.

Crests were meant to be displayed on top of a helm, and are so shown in the full achievement. It has become a common practice, however, to use crests on notepaper, signet rings, etc., without the arms and with the wreath conventionalised as a rigid bar underneath them. Sometimes, too, the crest and arms are shown without the helm. Lack of space or an unsuitable crest may sometimes make this convenient, but it is generally a mistake to abbreviate the achievement.

If an achievement has two crests they are normally placed on two separate helms, but some emblazonments of arms show them on either side of one helm, each with its own wreath beneath it. The crest of the senior coat goes on the dexter side and that of the junior coat on the sinister. In Scottish heraldry crests and helms are often turned to face each other (unless the crests are affronté). In English practice they both generally face to the dexter; for many English crests, owing to their unsuitable design, could not be turned round. If there are three crests, the one accompanying the senior coat is placed in the middle. Two crests often accompany a double surname, the additional name and arms having been acquired by Royal Licence or a Grant by Patent. Up till the beginning of the sixteenth century, however, crests could be inherited through heiresses in the same way as quarterings; and in Scotland, particularly in the early nineteenth century, crests have been granted to ladies "for behoof of their male issue". An additional crest is sometimes granted as an augmentation.

The use of the crest as a badge and the close relationship between the two will be dealt with in the chapter on badges.

THE HELM

The practical use and development of the helm has already been considered in Chapter II. The primary purpose of the helm in the achievement is to bear the crest; though it is not incorrect to use a helm if the arms do not possess a crest, and instances of such use can be seen in the Armorial de Gelre. The earliest appearance of helms on seals, however, does coincide with the earliest appearance of crests. Devices of various kinds had previously been shown on seals above the shield, but it was the presence of a helm supporting such a device which showed that it was a crest. The heraldic helm was not used, in the first instance, to indicate rank and it was generally in profile and of the pattern in actual use. The style of the latter half of the fourteenth century is shown in the Armorial de Gelre. (This armorial, to which several references have been and will be made, is a MS. in the Royal Library of Brussels. It is believed to be the work of Claes Heynen who was Gelre Herald to the Duke of Gueldres between 1334 and 1372, with some later additions by someone else. It includes paintings of more than 1800 shields and crests of the countries of Western Europe. There are 78 shields in the English section. The Scottish section is one of the principle authorities for early armory.) Although some earlier attempts were made to employ the helm as an indication of rank, the present system does not appear to have been used in England before the reign of Queen Elizabeth; and Scotland did not adopt it until after the union of the two crowns.

At present there are four different forms of helm. That borne by the Sovereign and the Royal Princes is gold, has grilles and is placed affronté. The peer's helm is silver with five golden grilles and is in profile. The helm of knights and baronets is affronté, of steel and has the visor open. Esquires and gentlemen have a steel helm in profile with a closed visor. In the achievement of Oliver Cromwell, as Lord Protector, his helm is blazoned as a "princely helmet of steel, burnished with gold". It is shown on his Great Seal as affronté with grilles. The buckler type of ceremonial helm is generally used for the Royal and peer's helms. The armet is the best pattern to show an open visor. The esquire's helm is well represented by either the jousting type with high eye-slit or the great helm. Silver and steel helms are generally garnished with gold. A

PLATE 14

SECOND FOLIO OF SCOTTISH ARMS IN THE ARMORIAL DE GELRE

Earl of Carrick	*Earl of Strathern*	*Earl of Atholl*	*Earl of Sutherland*	*Sir Archibald Douglas*
Earl of Orkney	*Lord of Seton*	*Earl of Ross*	*Sir Walter de Leslie*	*Sir John Stewart*
Sir James Lindsay	*Sir Alexander Stewart*	*Sir David Lindsay*	*Lord of Soulis*	*Sir John Abernethy*

well-proportioned helm can form a most attractive part of the achievement. Some most appalling little helms which could never have been worn will be seen on many representations of arms, particularly those of the mid-nineteenth century. These horrid excrescences are still, unfortunately, repeated to-day, even in some versions of the Royal Arms. The helm should conform to the same period as the shield and should not be too small. In his excellent book, *Scots Heraldry*, Thomas Innes of Learney suggests that a proportionate area of one-third each to shield, helm and crest would be appropriate, and adds that an allotment of one-half of the area to the shield and one-half to the helm and crest is the limit. The position rule is an unfortunate one and has some deplorable results. Animals passant appear, for instance, on affronté helms, and affronté crests are depicted on helms which are placed in profile. A certain amount can sometimes be done by twisting the helm slightly one way and the crest the other way. In Scottish armory the position rule has now, providentially, been dropped.

THE WREATH

The wreath, or torse, is a piece of twisted material which is worn round the helmet to hide the joint of crest and helm. In modern heraldry six twists or links are shown, and these are alternately the first-named metal and first-named colour in the blazon of the arms (known as "the Colours"). It is only in comparatively recent years that the number of twists has become universally standardised at six. As recently as 1820 in the Scottish grant to Sir Walter Scott the wreath had five twists, of which the two outside ones were metal. In English armory, however, it was an accepted rule by the middle of the sixteenth century that the wreath should start with a metal and end with a colour. The origin of the wreath is uncertain. Many writers have suggested that it represents the sleeve of a lady worn as a favour and twisted round the helm, and there is probably a great deal of truth in the theory. But it does not give the whole story. There are a number of peculiar wreaths surrounding the crests in the Armorial de Gelre, but none of them remotely resembles a lady's sleeve. The probability is, as Fox-Davies suggests, that originally a plain or ornamental fillet was worn round the crest, and when a lady's favour was displayed at tournaments it was twisted round and round the fillet. The fillet would be hidden by the favour and eventually it was probably replaced by a piece of twisted material which was very likely of the wearer's own livery colours. By the time Gerard Leigh wrote his *Accedens of Armory* in 1562, it was already the usual custom to use the colours of the paternal arms for the wreath.

As has already been said, it has become customary to show the wreath as a bar on which the crest stands when the latter is displayed by itself. There is a certain amount to be said for showing a wreath with a crest when used apart from the remainder of the achievement, since it differentiates it from a badge, but this method of drawing the wreath has resulted in some horrible examples of heraldic art in which a bar-like wreath is shown perched precariously on top of the helm.

THE CREST CORONET AND THE CHAPEAU

When a crest is shown issuing from a coronet, the latter is known as a crest coronet. Used as such, it has no connection with the coronet of rank (which is dealt with later). At one time a wreath was always placed below a crest coronet, but it never appears now unless particularly specified in the grant. The types of coronets used with crests include the ducal coronet, the mural coronet, the naval coronet, the Eastern coronet, the crown vallary, the palisado coronet and various other types which are of infrequent occurrence.

The ducal coronet is never granted now, though there are many examples in existence from ancient grants. As used with a crest, it differs from the ducal coronet of rank in that it has only three strawberry leaves instead of five, and no central cap or band of ermine below it. According to some old writers the qualification for the ducal crest coronet was descent from some ancestor who was in personal attendance on a sovereign at a coronation. They and the cadets of the Royal House were granted gold coronets, whilst their followers were allowed coronets of red, green or black. Examples of some of these can be seen in the folios of the Armorial de Gelre. A mural coronet is composed of masonry and is embattled at the top. It is often granted to distinguished officers of the army, from the old Roman custom of crowning the first soldier to climb the walls in the assault on a town or fortress, and occasionally, though officially not allowed, to borough and county councils. The naval coronet consists of a circlet on which sails and ships' sterns are set alternately. It is granted to admirals for distinguished service. The Eastern coronet has triangular spikes set dancetté fashion on a circlet. It is awarded for service in the East. The crown vallary has the rim set with vair-shaped pieces, and the palisado coronet has a series of perpendicular pieces with sharp points set to the rim. These last two are the only coronets now permissible for ordinary grants.

The chapeau is a peculiar headdress. It is alternatively known as the "cap of maintenance" or "cap of dignity". It is usually shown as a red velvet cap with an ermine turn-up split at the back into two short tails. The cap and lining are sometimes blazoned as of different tinctures. In England the chapeau is now confined to peers and their descendants.

82

In Scotland it has no official restriction, but has been little used outside a few families. The origin of the chapeau is obscure. The memorial brass of Henry, Duke of Lancaster, who died in 1347, shows him holding in his hand his great helm, on the top of which is a chapeau surmounted by the English Royal Crest of a crowned lion statant guardant. A mantling hangs down from underneath the chapeau over the back of the

Chapeau
or Cap *of* Dignity

Fig. VI

helm. The chapeau is of the same type as used in modern heraldic design, but the crown is higher and, as far as can be seen, it is not divided at the back. A similar chapeau appears on the seal of Thomas de Mowbray, Earl of Nottingham, 1389, and there is one on the helmet of the Black Prince preserved in Canterbury Cathedral. The cap of maintenance borne before the Sovereign at the State Opening of Parliament is of quite different design. It has a tall conical crimson crown and is lined with ermine. The chapeau, the Royal cap of maintenance and the caps which are worn inside crowns and coronets with an ermine turn-up, all probably owe their origin to some headdress which was used as an emblem of dignity.

THE MANTLING OR LAMBREQUIN

The "Mantling" or "Lambrequin" is the piece of cloth which hung down the back of the helmet to protect the back of the neck from the heat of the sun, fulfilling the same function as the short cotton curtain which was worn at the back of the tropical headdress of the British Army before the introduction of the topi. It originated as the "capeline", or helmet covering. When crests were introduced, the back of the crest, if its design permitted, was often intended to form the mantling. Many examples will be seen in the Armorial de Gelre folios, together with two helmets with capelines only and no crests. The borders are frequently cut into tongue-shaped pieces, which were a popular fourteenth-century ornamentation on surcoats and other garments. The Armorial de Gelre shows that there was often no connection between the colours of the arms and the colours of the mantling, and that, on the other hand, the arms were sometimes repeated on the mantling. Other examples of early mantling may be seen on several of the memorial brasses, notably those of the Black Prince (1376), Sir John de Foxley (1378), Henry, Duke of Lancaster (1347), Sir Humphrey Littlebury (*c.* Edward III), Ralph Nevill, Earl of Westmoreland (1425), Sir Edmund de Thorpe (1418) and Sir John de La Pole (1491). The fourteenth-century examples are similar to those shown in the Armorial de Gelre. The fifteenth-century ones, however, are in the form of a straight curtain with a level bottom edge and with tassels at each bottom corner.

In the sixteenth century mantling, as an ornamental design, began to appear on seals, filling the spaces between the shield and the annulus of the seal which had been previously occupied by diapering, foliage, etc. This is the origin of the slashed material curled into decorative patterns, and not the picturesque idea, which many writers (the present writer, alas, amongst them) have repeated, that the mantling is so represented because it was so often cut in battle. If anyone doubts this assertion let him place a hat on a peg, suspend a handkerchief from the back of the crown and attack it with a sword.

In the fifteenth century a mantling of "gules doubled argent" became increasingly popular, and by the sixteenth century it was practically universal and was generally so specified in the grant. Gold tassels sometimes accompanied this mantling. In England the livery colours of the arms were substituted in the seventeenth century, but in Scotland the gules and argent mantling was retained until 1890. Until fairly recent years in England the mantling of peers was lined with ermine, and this practice is still in force in Scotland, the colour being gules (though the wreath is of the ordinary livery colours). In England a modern official exemplification of an ancient grant depicts mantling in the livery colours even though gules and argent may have been originally granted. If two or more crests are shown on separate helms and if they are associated with different arms in a quartered coat, each mantling will display the livery colours of its own arms.

SUPPORTERS

Supporters (originally called "bearers" in Scotland), as their name implies, support or bear up a shield of arms. There may be one or two supporters. The latter are the most frequent and are generally human figures, beasts, monsters or birds. The most usual single supporter is the eagle displayed, or displayed with wings inverted. But such inanimate objects as a tree and the mast of an ancient ship are sometimes used.

As in the case of the mantling, supporters probably originated in the decoration of seals by engravers. A roughly triangular shield left a rather blank space between it and the annular of the seal. This space was variously ornamented with tracery, foliage, diapering and heraldic beasts. The first three, as we have already seen, were replaced by the mantling, and the last evolved into supporters. Dragons appear to have been the beasts in most common use as decoration, and sometimes three or four were placed round the shield. The advancement of these animals to the status of supporters seems to have followed the addition to the seal of the helm and crest at about the beginning of the fourteenth century. The shield on the seal of Henry of Lancaster, Earl of Derby (afterwards King Henry IV), is supported by two lions rampant guardant addorsed, and is held at the top by an angel. Although in many cases the supporters had no other origin than the fancy of the engraver, it is probable that, in the same way that a badge was selected as a crest, other badges were often chosen as supporters. Again, like crests, supporters were not originally regarded as hereditary and were frequently changed.

The right to bear supporters has been strictly limited since about the beginning of the sixteenth century. In England they are confined to peers, Knights of the Garter, Thistle and St. Patrick, Knights Grand Cross or Grand Commander of other orders, and public bodies. Baronets have in some cases been granted supporters, but they are not entitled to claim them. There are instances, too, of their grant to untitled persons as a mark of Royal favour or as an augmentation of honour. Some families claim supporters by prescriptive right, but official sanction has not been given to their use. The rules in Ireland are the same as in England, but in the Republic of Ireland "Chiefs of the Name" may now be granted supporters by the Chief Herald of Ireland. In earlier days they used them without authority from Ulster King of Arms. (The O'Connor Don, however, was granted supporters by a Royal Warrant issued by Queen Victoria on her last visit to Dublin.)

In Scotland, supporters are allowed to peers, heirs of lairds (or the minor barons) who sat in Parliament prior to 1587, chiefs of clans, certain knights who are entitled by right to obtain supporters and certain others by ancient usage. In addition the Lord Lyon has discretionary powers to grant supporters to any person on whom he elects to confer the honour. In Scotland (but not in England) an heir apparent may bear his father's supporters.

THE COMPARTMENT

The term "compartment" appears to have originated in Scottish heraldry. Its use is restricted to achievements having supporters and its main function is to provide them with something to stand on. It was supposed by some authorities to represent the land and territories of the owner of the arms. The compartment in Scottish heraldry is frequently shown as a grassy mound, and in recent years this practice has become increasingly popular in England. But in English armory the motto scroll was previously in almost universal use as a base for supporters, and to Guillim the terms "compartment" and "scroll" seem to have been synonymous. In modern armory the type and design of the compartment is left to the fancy of the artist, unless it is specifically mentioned in the blazon, and all kinds of compartments are now used—grassy mounds, rocks, sea, motto scrolls, gilt scrolls or "gas brackets", stone platforms, etc.

THE MOTTO

In English armory mottoes are not hereditary, no authority is needed for their adoption and the choice of a motto is left to individual taste. In the case of a grant of arms to a public body, however, a motto is sometimes included. In Scotland the motto is invariably made the subject of a grant and cannot be altered. There is, however, no property recognised in the motto taken by itself. The slogan, or war-cry, is often different to the motto, and in that case it is confined to the chief of the clan or house, and is generally shown in the achievement as a second motto. In Ireland the practice is a mixture of English and Scottish usage. Sometimes the motto is expressed in the patent and sometimes it is not. In England and Ireland the motto is generally placed below the arms and in Scotland above the crest.

THE ROBE OF ESTATE

A peer's robe of estate is sometimes seen as a background to the arms. This is of scarlet lined with taffeta. The different degrees of rank are shown by the guards or bands of fur. A duke's robe has four guards of ermine, with gold lace above each guard, and is tied up to the left shoulder with a white riband. The robe of a marquess has four guards of ermine on the right side and three on the left, with gold lace above each guard, and is also tied up to the left shoulder with a white riband. An earl's robe has three guards of ermine with gold lace. The robes of a viscount and a baron each have two guards of plain white fur.

Chapter IX

CROWNS AND CORONETS

ROWNS and coronets as emblems of sovereignty owe their origin to the fillets and diadems of antiquity. The fillet probably started as a piece of cloth tied round the head to keep long hair away from the eyes. From a purely utilitarian beginning it would naturally lend itself to ornamentation. The coloured ribbons and other hair ornaments worn by women provide a modern example of this early use. The next step in the development of the fillet, according to that great authority the late Mr. Cyril Davenport, F.S.A., was its specialisation. Priests, for instance, wore one pattern and fighting-men another. A similar example of such specialisation can be found to-day in the variously coloured bands worn round the forage and service-dress caps of the British Army. A further logical step would be the adoption by the chieftain or king of a special fillet for his own use. Mr. Davenport suggests that the use of a special colour to indicate authority probably originated in the East. Alexander the Great adopted it and used the diadem of the King of Persia. The ancient royal diadems were sometimes of a soft material and sometimes of metal. The diadem of the Roman Kings was the royal white ribbon which the Emperors dared not wear.

The early British Kings wore fillets of various kinds. Metal crowns were first worn in England by the Anglo-Saxon Kings, and consisted originally of a circlet with three vertical points, each topped with either one or three pearls. This type of crown was also placed on a helm to distinguish the King in battle. Canute introduced a new fashion and replaced the points with three trefoils. The earliest crown with arches seems to have been worn by King Edward the Confessor. It was of very simple design with a tassel hanging from each side. William the Conqueror apparently had two crowns. One of these was of the old Anglo-Saxon pattern with three points. The other had a broad rim and two shallow arches with pendants on each side. William II's crown was a circlet with five points and pendants. Henry I had a circlet with three fleurs-de-lis and pendants. Stephen's crown had three fleurs-de-lis and two arches. Henry II had a crown with jewelled rim and arches and a pendant at the back. Henry III's crown was ornamented with large fleurs-de-lis and bore a distinct resemblance to a modern crest coronet. Edward I used a similar crown, but the rim was broader and the fleurs-de-lis alternated with single pearls. The cross patée first appears in the crown of Henry VI. The arched crown of Edward IV was surmounted by the familiar symbol of the cross over the orb which is supposed to promise the maintenance of the Christian religion in the realm. The final form of the official crown of England was produced in the reign of Henry VIII. The rim is ornamented with alternate fleurs-de-lis and crosses patée and the arches are surmounted by the orb and cross. The description of these old English crowns is taken from seals and coins which show a conventionalised form. The number of points and other decorations on the actual crowns was certainly greater than here stated.

There are two crowns of England. The first is the official crown, known as St. Edward's Crown, and the second is the Imperial State Crown. The present St. Edward's Crown is of the same pattern as that made for the coronation of Charles II and is probably composed mainly of the same materials. Charles II's crown was very similar in design to its predecessor. The St. Edward's Crown consists of a gold circlet from which rise four crosses patée alternating with four fleurs-de-lis. Two gold arches intersect each other and are supported on the tops of the four crosses patée. The arches dip downwards to the point of inter-section, on which is a gold mound encircled by a fillet round its horizontal diameter and with its top banded vertically by a half fillet. The mound is surmounted by a gold cross patée. On the rim are white and red enamel arabesques, and these are set with rosettes of gems which have rubies, emeralds and sapphires in the centre and are surrounded by diamonds. Along the upper and lower edges of the circlet are rows of pearls. The crosses patée also bear white and red arabesques set with gems. The arches are edged with rows of pearls between which are gem-set white and red arabesques. The fillets of the mound are adorned with pearls and gems. The cross on the mound is set with gems, has one large pearl at the top and a pear-shaped pearl suspended from each end of the cross arm. A purple velvet cap turned up with miniver is worn inside the crown.

An heraldic representation of St. Edward's Crown is shown in achievements of the Royal Arms and is used on paper and in badges, etc. (including Army rank badges), for all official purposes. The crown as heraldically represented differs considerably from the actual article. It originated as a War Office sealed pattern early in the reign of King Edward VII. At that time there was considerable latitude in the drawing of the crown, and the opportunity was taken to notify His Majesty's pleasure that the War Office pattern should be adopted for official use. The cap of the heraldic crown is always shown as red turned up with ermine.

The St. Edward's Crown must be present at the Coronation, but the Imperial State Crown is the one which is actually worn on all State occasions. It follows the same general design as St. Edward's Crown, but it is remade for each Sovereign. In this crown are the really historic national jewels. These include: the great sapphire from the crown of King Charles II, which Cardinal York bequeathed to King George III; the great ruby of the King of Granada, murdered for the sake of it by Don Pedro, King of Castile, who presented it in gratitude for his assistance to the Black Prince, and which King Henry V is said to have worn in his crown at Agincourt; and the large sapphire from the ring of Edward the Confessor, Saint and King, the possession of which is said to confer the power of curing cramp. A purple velvet cap turned up with miniver is worn with the crown.

The coronet of the Prince of Wales, in his capacity as heir apparent, is of exactly the same design as the St. Edward's Crown except that the "fore-and-aft" arch is omitted. Heraldically it is normally depicted as similar to the "official" crown except for the omission of the one arch. Sometimes, however, it is drawn as heavily ornamented with pearls and with the arch dipped in the centre. The rules with regard to the coronets of other members of the Royal Family are rather complicated. They are:

1. The brothers, sisters, sons (other than the Prince of Wales) and daughters of a past or present Sovereign of Great Britain have a coronet which is the same as that of the Prince of Wales except that it has no arch and the cap is surmounted by a tassel.

2. The grandchildren of a past or present Sovereign of Great Britain who are sons and daughters of any of his sons, and who are in the direct line, have a similar type of a coronet, but strawberry leaves are substituted for two of the crosses patée (the dexter and sinister ones in the heraldic drawing).

3. Princes of the Royal Family who are sons of younger sons of a past or present Sovereign or who are sons of the Sovereign's brothers and having the rank and title of a duke of the United Kingdom have a coronet composed of alternate crosses patée and strawberry leaves.

4. The grandchildren of a past or present Sovereign who are sons and daughters of any of his daughters with the style of "Highness" have a coronet composed of alternate fleurs-de-lis and strawberry leaves.

These coronets are assigned by Royal Warrant with the arms and are not inherited as a matter of right.

Although the use of coronets by peers in accordance with their rank had been customary since the reign of Queen Elizabeth (dukes had worn them first in the time of Edward III), it was not till the reign of King Charles II that peers who were not of the Blood Royal had coronets assigned to them by Royal Warrant. The patterns previously in use, however, were retained, and barons, who had previously been omitted, had a coronet assigned to them. All the coronets are of silver gilt with crimson velvet caps turned up with ermine and surmounted with a gold tassel. No jewels or stones are allowed to be set in them and counterfeit pearls are not allowed to be used instead of silver balls. The coronets of a duke, marquess, an earl and a viscount have chased circlets, whilst the circlet of a baron's coronet is plain. The duke's coronet has eight gold strawberry leaves, of which five are shown in heraldic representations.

| Baron | Viscount | Earl | Marquess | Duke |

Fig. VII.—CORONETS

The coronet of a marquess has four gold strawberry leaves alternating with four silver balls raised on points slightly above the rim. In the heraldic coronet three strawberry leaves and two pearls (instead of silver balls) are shown. An earl's coronet has eight silver balls raised upon lofty spikes with eight gold strawberry leaves between them. In the heraldic version these become five pearls on tall spikes and four strawberry leaves. The coronet worn by a viscount has sixteen silver balls set on the rim, and nine pearls are set closely together in the representation. A baron's coronet has six silver balls, and the heraldic drawing shows four large pearls on the top edge of the circlet. Sometimes, in heraldic representations, the velvet cap of the peer's coronet is omitted.

The crown of a King of Arms is silver gilt with sixteen leaves set on the rim. The leaves are alternately tall and short. The cap is of crimson satin with a gold tassel on top and is turned up with ermine. The circlet is inscribed with part of the 50th Psalm (or, according to the Authorised Version, the 51st Psalm): "Miserere mei, Deus, Secundum magnam misericordiam tuam" ("Have mercy on me, O God, as thou art ever rich in mercy"). On the representation of this crown there are five tall leaves and four short leaves, and the words, "Miserere mei, Deus" appear on the circlet.

Chapter X

AUGMENTATIONS, ABATEMENTS, BASTARDY

"AUGMENTATIONS of Honour" are marks of Royal favour, "Abatements of Honour" are marks indicating a stain on the honour of the bearer, and "Marks of Bastardy" are self-explanatory.

AUGMENTATIONS OF HONOUR

Augmentations of Honour are awarded for distinguished service in war or peace and are the most prized additions to an achievement of arms. They are granted by the King, as an especial mark of favour, and under a Royal Warrant, instead of by the Officer of Arms. An augmentation generally takes one or more of the following forms:

1. *A second shield of arms to quarter with the paternal coat.* Dr. Edward Lake was awarded a quartering by King Charles I in recognition of his gallantry at the Battle of Naseby. Sir John de Pelham, for his service at the Battle of Poictiers, received a quartering which included two buckles and thongs, representing the sword belt of the captured French King.

2. *Additional charges.* Sir Cloudesley Shovel was given two crescents to commemorate two victories over the Turks and one fleur-de-lis for a victory over the French.

3. *A canton.* The Lane family was granted a canton of the Arms of England in reward for the gallantry of Mistress Jane Lane in assisting King Charles II to escape from England. The King accompanied Mistress Lane on horseback disguised as her servant. King Charles II awarded Winston Churchill, father of the Duke of Marlborough, a canton of the Cross of St. George.

4. *An escutcheon.* The Duke of Marlborough received a second augmentation to the Churchill arms from Queen Anne for his great victory of Blenheim. This was an escutcheon, again of the Cross of St. George but charged with a second escutcheon of the arms of France, and borne on the honour point. An award of an augmentation to both father and son is probably unique in heraldry. The Duke of Wellington was granted an escutcheon of the Union, also borne on the honour point.

5. *A pile.* For smashing the Khalifa, Lord Kitchener was given a pile charged with the Union and Egyptian flags.

6. *A bordure.* Edward VI granted a bordure charged with lion's gambs to Lord Wharton for " cutting the claws" of the Scottish Lion at the Battle of Solway Moss.

7. *A chief.* The two famous surgeons, Sir Frederick Treves, Bart., and Sir Francis Laking, Bart., were each awarded a red chief charged with a lion of England for the services they rendered to King Edward VII when he was taken ill at the time of his coronation.

8. *An additional crest.* The Lanes of Kings Bromley were awarded as a crest the strawberry roan horse on which the King and Mistress Jane had ridden, couped at the flanks and holding in its fore feet the Royal crown. Capt. Broke, the victor in the celebrated battle between the *Shannon* and the *Chesapeake*, was awarded a crest of an arm issuing from a naval crown and holding a trident accompanied by the motto "Saevamque tridentem servamus".

9. *Supporters.* For his victory at Solway Moss, Lord Wharton also received a "lion gules, fretty or" as a sinister supporter. In other words, the Scottish lion in a net.

In addition to their award for distinguished service, augmentations have sometimes, in the past, been granted to favourites or relations of the King as a mere favour. Richard II was particularly addicted to this method of rewarding his intimates, and Henry VIII seems to have regarded it as a convenient, if inexpensive, way of providing presents for his wives.

ABATEMENTS OF HONOUR

According to Guillim, an abatement of honour indicated "some ungentlemanlike, dishonourable or disloyal demeanour, quality or stain in the Bearer whereby the Dignity of the Coat Armour is greatly abased". He lists the following acts as warranting an abatement: revoking a challenge, treating women discourteously, running away, boasting of military prowess, slothfulness in war, killing a prisoner, lying, cowardice and treachery. For the last-mentioned crime the arms were reversed, and, after the execution of their owner, they were forfeited for ever and erased from the records of the College of Arms. His descendants, if they were deemed suitable to bear arms, would have to obtain an entirely new grant. For the other offences Guillim lists a number of sub-ordinaries, not otherwise used in English armory, with which the shield of arms was debruised. The tincture was always one of the stains, that is, tenné or sanguine. For example a "point champaine tenné" was awarded for killing a prisoner who had yielded, and a "point in point sanguine" for sloth in war. (A point champaine is an ordinary in the base of the shield, the top of which is formed by the convex arc of a circle. A point in point is like a pile issuing from the base with concave curved sides, and the apex resting on the honour point.)

Most heraldic authorities deny the existence of these abatements and maintain that they were invented by the old heralds. Fox-Davies even refers to them as "one of those pleasant little insanities which have done so much to the detriment of heraldry". It has been stated that there is no known case of a mark of abatement ever having been used, and it is contended that a man would refrain from bearing arms at all rather than so advertise his dishonour. On the other hand, Guillim was a Pursuivant of Arms and a very eminent authority. It is hardly likely that he would invent a system of abatements. Furthermore, as Sir Christopher and Mr. Adrian Lynch-Robinson have pointed out, nobody is likely to advertise the fact that either he or one of his ancestors ever received a mark of abatement, and, if a Sovereign of the Middle Ages had ordered a knight to bear arms with a mark of abatement, it is hardly likely that the same knight would dare to appear with plain surcoat and shield. In any case, Guillim states that a plain white shield was borne by novices in martial affairs, known as "Freshwater Souldiers". The Lynch-Robinsons, too, cite four instances of abatements of arms which have been given by early authorities. It seems possible that Guillim set out a code which had already fallen into disuse at the time that he wrote, but which may well have been in active use during the great days of chivalry.

BASTARDY

For some extraordinary reason the only heraldic knowledge which many people possess is that a distinctive mark may be placed on arms to denote illegitimacy. Even more extraordinary is the fact that this mark is known to the same people as a "bar sinister". The reader will be aware that since a bar is horizontal it can neither be dexter nor sinister, and, furthermore, that a bar is never borne singly. Yet surprisingly enough the term "bar sinister" still appears in books the authors of which have obviously taken considerable pains that the other matters on which they write shall be exact and accurate. In all probability "bar sinister" has its origin in the French "barre"; for "barre" in French armory is a bend sinister, and a bend sinister was in fact used as a mark of bastardy.

It may seem strange in these days that anyone should choose to advertise the fact of illegitimate birth; but up till fairly recent years it was not regarded as of very great moment, and if the father was of Royal birth or one of the great peers of the realm it was even something to boast about. In the Middle Ages it was of no importance at all, and illegitimate sons sometimes succeeded to estates and titles in preference to relations of legitimate descent.

Originally there were no marks of bastardy. Their use probably arose of necessity when a man had both legitimate and illegitimate off-spring and it was desired to show that the latter and their descendants were debarred from inheritance. Even so, there was at this stage no distinction between the methods of differencing the paternal arms used by younger sons and those employed by their illegitimate half-brothers. Such distinction first arose in England when the present cadency marks replaced the use of ordinaries, tinctures, etc., to difference the arms of cadet lines. In Scotland cadency and bastardy were similarly treated until a much later date.

Although the arms of bastards were marked as if they were younger sons, certain ordinaries gradually came into increasingly common use. The two most often employed were the bend and its diminutives and the bordure. At a later stage the bend sinister appeared and probably gave rise to the term "left-handed marriage". At about the end of the fourteenth century Royal bastards sometimes showed their fathers' arms on ordinaries such as a bend, fess, etc. From the bend sinister was derived the baton, and by the time Guillim wrote in the early seventeenth century the baton was the normal mark of bastardy in English armory. Batons might be of any colour, but metal ones were reserved for those of Royal birth. The bordure wavy first appeared at the end of the eighteenth century, and since then it has become the usual mark of illegitimacy in England, though the metal baton is still retained for Royal bastards. In Scotland the bordure compony is always used, but it does not necessarily indicate bastardy. In England, but not in Scotland, a mark of distinction is now also placed on the crest. This is usually a scarp wavy, but a pallet wavy and a saltire wavy are also sometimes used. Irish practice has been the same as English, but some exemplifications issued by Ulster King of Arms have had the crest charged with a baton.

It should be noted that a cadency mark is a "mark of difference", whereas a mark of bastardy is termed a "mark of distinction".

Under the present law an illegitimate child has no surname at birth and does not inherit arms. There is no right, therefore, to bear paternal arms with a mark of distinction. If a person of illegitimate birth wishes to bear his father's arms he must first produce indisputable proof of his parentage. In England he then petitions the Sovereign for a Royal Licence to use the name and bear the arms of his father. In Scotland and in the Republic of Ireland bastardy is a matter for the Lord Lyon and the Chief Herald respectively. The arms when exemplified will be given a mark of distinction.

Chapter XI

THE BADGE

T HE term "badge" is one of the most elastic in heraldry, and no official definition of a badge has yet been produced. It would probably be reasonably accurate to say that a badge is an emblem which is associated with, but not part of, an achievement of arms and which is officially recognised. Any emblem which is not included in this definition we might call a "device". The badges of the Army, for instance, are properly so called because they are associated with the Royal Arms. The scaly beast worn on the caps of Little Puddlington Grammar School, on the other hand, is very likely a device.

In the early days of heraldry families seem to have adopted various symbols in addition to their armorial bearings. In some cases they may have been used purely ornamentally on seals and property, in others they may have served to difference a man's seal from that of his father. Such devices were changed at will and had no hereditary significance. Once a device of this nature acquired some sentimental association, it would tend to become hereditary and acquire the status of a badge, as we understand it to-day.

We have seen how there is reason to suppose that both crest and supporters owe their origin to the use of family badges. It is possible, too, that some badges originated in the beasts with which the seal engraver sometimes filled the gap between the shield and the annular of the seal. Many famous badges, however, were already old at the dawn of heraldry. The emblem of St. George and the Dragon, for instance, which is a badge of the Order of the Garter, has a very ancient history. In the matchless words of Mr. Walter de Gray Birch in his book *Seals*, "The Abbess Matildis, early in the thirteenth century, had a ring set with an oval gem, as ancient as the first years of the Christian epoch, bearing the engraving of St. George on a horse, attacking the dragon with a long spear. This legend, like some others now unfortunately considered idle and childish fables, is really a survival of oral tradition handed down from the far-off paleontozoic period, when the human animal, emerging into manship and divinely taught, strove with the monster Saurians of the now extinct past for a place upon the earth, and became paramount by reason of the divine afflatus which the Creator had breathed into his handiwork." The eagle of the Roman Legions is a badge of two regiments of the

British Army, and the shamrock badge of Ireland was St. Patrick's example of the Holy Trinity. As will be seen later on, there has been a great deal of overlapping as regards the use of badge and crest, but whereas a crest should be capable of being modelled "in the round", a badge need not be.

THE GREAT FAMILIES

It was not till the reign of Edward III that the badge seems to have become an important factor in heraldry, and it owed its rapid growth in importance and popularity to the same reasons which are responsible for its widespread use to-day. The badge was not worn by its owner, for he had his own personal arms. It served to distinguish his servants and retainers in peace and war, as an emblem of his party (if he was a powerful noble), as a rallying-point on the battlefield and as a distinctive mark on his property.

The badges of the great families in England reached their greatest importance at the time of the Wars of the Roses, when they were worn by the soldiers of the various private armies. The foundation of a standing army by Henry VII was followed by the disappearance of these baronial forces, and the family badge subsided into comparative obscurity. In their heyday the badges of the principal families were so well known that the head of a family was frequently referred to by the name of his badge. The bear and ragged staff of the Beauchamps, which Warwick "the Kingmaker" acquired from his heiress wife, was one of the most famous badges of the Wars of the Roses. It now appears as a charge in the Arms of Warwickshire County Council and as the cap badge of the Warwickshire Yeomanry. The white swan of the de Bohuns, which surmounts the shield on the seal of Humphrey de Bohun, Earl of Hereford, who died in 1298, was adopted by Edward, Duke of Cornwall, son of Henry VI, during the Wars of the Roses by virtue of his de Bohun great-grandmother. The Staffords, Dukes of Buckingham, acquired it by descent and it is now borne in the arms of the Borough of Buckingham. The numerous "White Swan" public houses owe the origin of their name and sign to the ancient badge of the de Bohuns. The Stafford knot, another badge of the Stafford family, is a badge of the South Staffordshire Regiment, the North Staffordshire Regiment (The Prince of Wales's) and the Staffordshire Yeomanry (Queen's Own Royal Regiment). It also appears in the Arms of the Borough of Stafford and the Staffordshire County Council. The portcullis of the Beauforts and Nevilles is a charge in the arms of the Marquess of Abergavenny and also of the Borough of Abergavenny and the City of Westminster. It is the badge of Portcullis Pursuivant, the Royal Gloucestershire Hussars

PLATE 15

THIRD FOLIO OF SCOTTISH ARMS IN THE ARMORIAL DE GELRE

Top:	Sir James Sandelands of Calder	Sir Robert of Erskin	Lord of Moray	Sir Thomas of Erskine	Lord of Keith
Centre:	Sir Alexander Ramsay	Sir John of Edmonston	Sir Robert Colville	Sir Walter Halyburton	Sir Harry of Preston
Bottom:	Sir — Comyn	Sir John St. Clair	— Craig	Sir Patrick Hepburn	—

and part of the cap badge of the Queen's Westminsters (The King's Royal Rifle Corps).

From past usage it would appear that badges descend in the same way as quarterings, though nothing as yet has been officially laid down. The Stafford badges as exemplified to the Earl of Stafford in 1720 numbered no less than eighteen. Each of the badges in this exemplification is shown upon a coloured roundel, though it is not clear as to whether family badges should always be borne in this manner. The Stafford knot is shown as gold on an escutcheon per pale sable and gules, which in turn is borne on a roundel *vert*. Three of the badges, the swan amongst them, have an additional peculiarity in that they are mounted on wreaths as if they were crests, which seems to point to the early interchangeability of crests and badges.

ROYAL AND NATIONAL BADGES

The earliest Royal badge, in the modern meaning of the term, is probably the roundel charged with a sixfoil, which is engraved on either side of the throne on the Great Seal of King William II. It was probably originally introduced to difference his seal from that of his father, but it appears frequently on contemporary Norman architecture. This emblem became known later as the "sixfoil rose-en-soleil". On King Stephen's Great Seal there is an estoile of seven points above the King's head, and this estoile appears again on the first seal of King Richard I together with a crescent. This seal also displays the sprigs of broom, the "planta genista" after which the Plantagenets have been named and which he inherited from his father. On Richard's second seal the crescent has become a full moon and the estoile a sun. It has been suggested that the estoile was really meant to be a sun, and that the sun and moon are the symbols of watchfulness by day and night. Other theories link them with the Crusades.

The most famous of all English Royal badges is the rose. The first rose was a golden one and was brought from Provence by Eleanor, Queen of Henry III. Edward I adopted it as a badge, whilst his youngest brother Edmund "Crouchback", Earl of Lancaster, also assumed a rose as a badge, but coloured his red. The gold rose remained a Royal badge till the death of Richard II, when the House of Lancaster brought its own red rose to the Throne of England. The white rose was a badge of Roger Mortimer, Earl of March and Heir Apparent to Richard II. His daughter married into the House of York and was grandmother of King Edward IV. After the Yorkist victory at Towton and his own coronation, Edward IV placed the white rose on the old Royal badge of the sun in commemoration of his success. The combination became known as the "white rose-en-soleil". The white rose-en-soleil played a notable part in the Battle of Barnet, where Warwick "the Kingmaker" and his ally de Vere opposed Edward IV. De Vere's troops were wearing his own white star (which is the sole charge in the de Vere arms). Warwick's men mistook this for the rose-en-soleil and charged their own side. The result was a Yorkist victory and the death of Warwick. Henry VII, the ultimately victorious red-rose champion, married the heiress of the House of York and united the rival Houses. An outcome of this union is the well-known Tudor red and white rose which is the badge of England to-day. The white rose, which had represented legitimism in the civil wars, was subsequently adopted as a badge by the Jacobites, who founded the still existing Order of the White Rose. The separate red and white roses are now badges of Lancashire and Yorkshire regiments and appear frequently in the civic arms of the two counties.

Another well-known badge is the ostrich-feather plume of the Heir Apparent. The origin of this is doubtful, but it seems most likely that Phillipa of Hainault, Queen of King Edward III, introduced the feathers, and that they alluded to the County of Ostrevant, which was an appanage of the Counts of Hainault. In any case, Edward, Prince of Wales (the "Black Prince"), adopted a black shield charged with three silver ostrich feathers as his arms "for peace". It was probably from his black jupon embroidered with the ostrich feathers that he received his descriptive title. In their present form the three feathers are, of course, grouped together in a plume with a scroll bearing the ancient motto, "Ich dien".

A favourite badge of Richard II was a white hart, which is still commemorated in the names and signs of countless inns. Another Royal badge which still exists in inn signs is the white boar of Richard III.

Partisan badges had a brief revival in England during the troubled years of the Reformation. Queen Mary adopted the badges of her mother, Queen Catherine, a pomegranate and a bundle of arrows, each dimidiated with the Tudor Rose by Henry VIII. These became the emblems of the English Catholics. The Protestants assumed the silver falcon holding a sceptre which had belonged to Anne Boleyn.

The earliest Scottish Royal badge seems, strangely enough, to have been a trefoil. A trefoil slipped appears frequently in Scottish Royal seals about the time of Alexander III. The backgrounds of both the obverse and reverse of the Great Seals of Alexander III and of the first Interregnum, before the accession of John Balliol, are semé of trefoils. On Alexander's seal two lizards, or wyverns, beneath the feet of the enthroned monarch, have tails which terminate in trefoils. The thistle appears for the first time on the second Great Seal of Robert Bruce in 1318.

Ireland has two badges, the harp and the shamrock. The crowned harp is first seen on Henry VIII's Irish groat. The ancient origin of the shamrock as a badge has already been mentioned. On the seal of Donat Macmuracha Da, King of Leinster in the fifteenth century, however, there are cinquefoils; though these are borne on trefoiled spandrels. James I's first Irish Seal includes a flag charged with a cross patée fitchée which, it has been suggested, represents a shamrock.

Following the union of the two crowns of England and Scotland the rose and thistle were united as a joint emblem. At first they were dimidiated, but since the reign of Queen Anne they have always been shown as separate flowers growing from the same stalk. Later the shamrock was added to the communal stalk, and in recent years the Welsh daffodil has joined the other three on a design used by H.M. Stationery Office. Floral emblems for the remaining two Celtic nations, Cornwall and the Isle of Man, have not so far been added! The daffodil is a fairly modern Welsh emblem. Wales has two very ancient badges in the leek and the red dragon. Tradition has it that Cadwallader, at the instigation of St. David, ordered his troops to wear leeks in their caps as a distinctive mark in battle. Some people maintain, however, that the daffodil, or "St. Peter's Leek", is the real Welsh vegetable. The red dragon was probably originally gold, and it is blazoned gold as a badge of the Welsh Guards. The golden dragon, the standard of Wessex, was the centre of the last stand at Hastings by the English "house carles", Harold's personal troops. But the dragon was far older than Hastings. The Emperor Trajan, when waging war in Gurgistan, captured a standard showing a dragon struck down by a horseman (St. George and the Dragon again). He took the dragon as his ensign, and it was hoisted all over the Empire. The Britons adopted it and fought under the dragon against the Saxon invaders. The Saxons, therefore, probably assumed the standard of their erstwhile enemies.

BADGES IN HER MAJESTY'S FORCES

It was the necessity of war which gave birth to heraldry, and so it is only to be expected that the greatest practical, as opposed to decorative, use of armorial insignia should be found in the fighting services.

When the Wars of the Roses came to an end with the death of Richard III on the field of Bosworth, a band of men, who had shared Henry Tudor's exile and who had played a major share in his victory, were formed into a personal bodyguard of the King and known as the "Yeomen of the Guard". In the new guard lay the seeds of a standing army and its formation presaged the extinction of the private forces of the great feudal lords. The State dress of the Yeomen of the Guard (commonly known as "Beefeaters") is scarlet and is embroidered back

PLATE 16

BADGES OF THE BRITISH ARMY

Fig. 1

THE LANCASHIRE FUSILIERS

Fig. 2

THE ROYAL FUSILIERS
(City of London
Regiment)

Fig. 3

THE COLDSTREAM
GUARDS
*The Star of the Order of
the Garter.*

Fig. 4

THE SHERWOOD FORESTERS
(Nottinghamshire · and
Derbyshire Regiment)
*A Maltese Cross charged
in the centre with a stag
lodged on water within a
wreath of oak.*

Fig. 5

THE BLACK WATCH
(Royal Highland Regi-
ment)
*The badge is a combina-
tion of the Star and Jewel
of the Order of the
Thistle.*

Fig. 6

THE ROYAL SCOTS
(The Royal Regiment)

*The Star of the Order of
the Thistle.*

Fig. 7

THE IRISH GUARDS
*The Star of the Order of
St. Patrick.*

Fig. 8

THE SEAFORTH
HIGHLANDERS
(Ross-shire Buffs, the
Duke of Albany's)
*The badge is ensigned
with the Cypher and
Coronet of the late Duke
of Albany.*

Fig. 9

THE ROYAL ULSTER
RIFLES

and front with the badge of the United Kingdom, the crowned and united rose, thistle and shamrock, flanked with the letters E. and R. The uniform is the same as in the days of King Henry VIII, but the badge, of course, has changed. The method of wearing the badge is probably very similar to the way retainers and servants wore the badge of their lord.

The Regular Army was not founded until the reign of King Charles II. Various badges were used by the regiments of the Army from an early date both on the Colours and uniform. The crest of the colonel of the regiment was sometimes worn as a badge with uniform. Royal regiments generally seem to have worn the Royal cypher and crown. Company Colours were particularly rich in badges. (Colours are dealt with in detail in the chapter on Flags.) Few of these early badges lasted, but by the middle of the eighteenth century several of the badges with which we are familiar to-day had appeared on Colours, and by the end of the century some of them were being worn on various items of uniform.

Most regiments of the Army to-day possess more than one badge, and the badge which is worn on the uniform frequently does not appear on the Colours. Many of these badges are of great historic interest and the majority are beautiful examples of heraldic art. The most common badge, strangely enough, is not British at all. It is the Egyptian sphinx and is borne by two regiments of horse and twenty-eight regiments of foot (including two of the disbanded infantry regiments from Southern Ireland). The Irish Royal badge of the harp and crown belongs to most of the Irish regiments. Several regiments have the Union rose (including, of course, the York and Lancaster Regiment), whilst the separate red and white roses are badges of many Lancashire and Yorkshire regiments respectively. The Life Guards and the Royal Horse Guards use the complete Royal achievement as a badge, and it is also one of the badges of the Royal Regiment of Artillery and the Corps of Royal Engineers. The 10th Royal Hussars (Prince of Wales's Own) and the 12th Royal Lancers (Prince of Wales's) both have the ostrich plume of the Heir Apparent, the rising sun, and the red dragon. The badge of the Royal Corps of Signals is the figure of Mercury ensigned with the Imperial Crown.

The King's Own Royal Regiment (Lancaster) wear the Lion of England. St. George and the Dragon is one of the badges of the Royal Northumberland Fusiliers. The Royal Inniskilling Fusiliers bear "The Castle of Inniskilling with three turrets and St. George's Colours flying". The badge borne on the Regimental Colour of the Duke of Cornwall's Light Infantry includes "The Castle and Lion as shown in the Great Seal of the Duchy of Cornwall". The Duke of Wellington's Regiment

(West Riding) uses the crest and motto of the Duke of Wellington. The rose and thistle on the same stalk within the garter, ensigned with the Imperial Crown, is a badge of the Welch Regiment. The Manchester Regiment has the fleur-de-lis. The badges of the Argyll and Sutherland Highlanders (Princess Louise's) include "A boar's head with the motto 'Ne obliviscusis' within a wreath of myrtle, and a cat with the motto 'Sans Peur' within a wreath of broom". (The myrtle and broom are Highland clan badges.)

That heraldry still fulfils a requirement in war is shown by the so-called "formation signs" that have been used during the last two great conflicts and appear to have become a permanent feature of the Army in peace. These are devices which have been adopted for divisions, corps, other formations, army commands, etc. In addition to other uses, they are worn on the sleeves of the battledress uniform. Many of them are heraldic in design and tinctures, and they emphasise the practical value that symbols still have. Furthermore, these cloth emblems sewn on to uniform probably bear a very close relationship to the badges sewn on to the dress of the men-at-arms in the feudal armies.

A very attractive series of badges were designed and drawn for the Royal Navy by Major Charles ffoulkes, F.S.A. Each badge consists of a coloured field with one or more charges, within a circular frame. The frame is surmounted by a naval coronet, below which is the name of the ship. The badge is placed on the quarterdeck together with a scroll of battle honours of the ship and of her predecessors of the same name. Each of the ship's boats bears a small replica of the badge.

Recently badges have been designed for squadrons of the Royal Air Force.

BADGES IN SCOTLAND

The position of the badge in Scotland differs from that of the remainder of the United Kingdom. In Scotland the badge is frequently synonymous with the crest, and the latter is often used as a badge when depicted without a helm. It is sometimes worn as a cap badge with Highland dress within a belt and buckle on which the motto is displayed. This is the conventionalised form of plate and strap within which clansmen bore the Chief's badge. (In England the Scottish belt and buckle would be called a garter, and its use is confined to Knights of the Garter.) If the crest is displayed on the helm, with or without belt and buckle, it shows that it is personal to the bearer and is not being worn as a badge. The Gordon Highlanders wear the crest of the Marquess of Huntly as a badge within a wreath of the clan ivy and surmounted by the motto "Bydand". Another species of badge is used by Highlanders as a mark of clanship. A leaf or sprig of a tree or shrub is worn on the coat or on the bonnet. The Campbells, for instance, use white myrtle; the Buchanans, bilberry; the Grahams, laurel; the Macdonalds, heath; the Sinclairs, gorse; the Murrays, butcher's broom; and the Gordons, ivy.

LIVERY

Livery colours to-day are normally the first metal and the first colour to be mentioned in the blazon of the arms, but this was by no means always the case in the past. The Royal livery colours were changed frequently up till the beginning of the seventeenth century. The Plantagenets' colours were white and scarlet; the House of Lancaster used white and blue; the Yorkists, murrey and blue; the Tudors, white and green. The Stuarts and all succeeding sovereigns have used gold and scarlet as their dress colour, and scarlet and blue as the undress. William III's colours were blue and orange before coming to the throne. Since early days it was the custom to dress servants and retainers in livery colours. Scarlet and blue has been for many years the traditional dress of the British Army and it is still retained in a modified form. Since the Queen's servants wear the Queen's livery, it would probably be correct to add Royal Air Force Blue to the livery colours. Owing to the Royal use of scarlet, a person or corporate body having red as one of the colours and wealthy enough to keep servants and dress them in livery would normally use some such colour as claret, mulberry or even chocolate.

There are various other permissible variations for the livery colours for undress or everyday use. Brown may be used instead of yellow, grey or light brown instead of white, and navy blue for azure. There are no regulations as to how the colours should be used in a uniform, but it is generally considered that for a full dress uniform the coat should be the tincture of the field and the trousers and waistcoat that of the principal charge. For everyday wear the most serviceable arrangement would be to have coat, waistcoat and trousers the "colour" of the livery and use the "metal" for facings, e.g. cuffs and collar. The buttons should be of the metal. It appears to be an established custom to have the crest engraved, mounted or stamped on the buttons, but a badge is much the more correct emblem if one is possessed.

Scottish tartans, which may be worn by anyone who is a member of the appropriate clan, are a form of livery colour; and the use of tartans by Scottish regiments, incidentally, is an example of the retention in the Army of private liveries and a reminder of the days when the Sovereign called upon his principal subjects to provide troops.

Chapter XII

ARMORIAL FLAGS

THE use of armorial bearings on flags followed rapidly on their adoption on shield and surcoat. It was a natural development that commanders at all levels in the chain of command should display their personal insignia on banners to act as a rallying mark in war. These banners, too, were almost essential to the Earl Marshal in his task of marshalling the army into its order of battle.

Banners, originally, were usually square, though sometimes their depth was greater than their width. They were charged with the arms of their owner in exactly the same way as a shield; the dexter side being regarded as that next to the staff. Animals, etc., which faced to the dexter, therefore, faced the staff on both sides of the flag. Banners could not normally be borne by any person in a degree lower than knight banneret. Ordinary knights with their retainers followed somebody else's banner, and at the siege of Carlaverock in 1300 there was one banner to every twenty-five or thirty men. Knights carried a pennon, a small swallow-tailed flag, attached to the lance head. This was emblazoned either with the arms of its owner or his badge, in such a way that they were upright when the lance was held in the horizontal position. When a knight was made a banneret on the field of battle, the tails of his pennon were ceremonially cut off, thereby converting it technically into a banner. Esquires seem to have used a triangular-shaped pennon known as a penoncel or pensil. These small flags have their modern equivalent in the pennons which are flown on the cars of commanders in the Army of to-day, charged with the badges of the formations which they command. British Army pennons are rectangular, swallow-tailed and triangular, in descending order, according to the importance of the command. The regulations regarding the use of pennons, in mediaeval days, however, seemed to have varied. A fifteenth-century MS., for instance, says that every knight should have his pennon, and should set his arms on it if he were a "chief captain". If he were made a banneret "he should slit it at the fly". Banners at this time seemed to have been restricted to barons.

At sea the sails of ships were frequently emblazoned with arms, and the pennon became a long whip-like flag. The latter, of course, is still used; and though it is spelt "pendant" is pronounced "pennant".

According to early regulations, the banner of the Sovereign was five foot square, that of a duke four foot square, and the banners of other nobles three foot square.

The standard was a much bigger flag than the banner; hence its name, for the staff to which it was attached was stuck in the ground instead of being carried about. It was the flag under which an overlord commanded his retainers in battle. (The present "Royal Standard", incidentally, is really a Royal Banner.) Originally the term "standard" did not necessarily mean a flag at all. The standards of the Roman legions, for instance, consisted of emblems mounted on the tops of staves. Later any large flag placed in a fixed position was called a standard. At the famous Battle of the Standard in 1138 between English and Scots there were actually three flags present: those of the patron saints of York, Beverley and Ripon. The English army had been raised by the Archbishop of York, and these were his three minster churches. The three standards were hoisted on one staff, which was mounted on a wagon of sorts and surmounted by the Host in a silver pyx. This battle took place, of course, in the years immediately preceding the birth of heraldry.

The heraldic standard came into very extensive use in the fifteenth century. It was a long tapering flag frequently slit at the fly, with the arms of the patron saint of the country in the portion immediately next to the staff. The remainder of the flag consisted of the livery colour or colours (parted per fess if there were two), on which were embroidered the badges (and sometimes the crest) and the motto or slogan in bendwise bands. Round the edge of the whole flag there was generally a fringe of the livery colours. The Sovereign's standard was eight yards in length, a duke's seven yards, a marquess's six and a half yards, an earl's six yards, a viscount's five and a half yards, a baron's five yards, a knight-baronet's four and a half yards and a knight's four yards. English standards had the red cross of St. George on a silver field next to the staff, and the Kings from Edward III to Henry VIII charged their livery colours with the Royal motto and their respective badges. Scottish standards were either of the livery colours of their owner or green, the colour of the national badge, the thistle. The cross of St. Andrew was placed next to the staff.

The guidon (from the French "guide-homme") was of later introduction and was rather an odd flag. It was rounded at the fly and sometimes slit, and was supposed to be one-third shorter than the standard. It bore its owner's complete achievement of arms (except for supporters) and his badges.

NATIONAL FLAGS

The Kings of England were already fighting under the banner of St. George, patron of England, by the first half of the thirteenth century;

and in the fourteenth century a surcoat emblazoned with the arms of the saint, argent, a cross gules was worn by every English soldier. The Scottish Kings similarly led their armies to war under the emblem of their own patron, St. Andrew; and his banner, *Azure, a saltire argent*, was, and still is, greatly venerated. In neither country, however, was there any particular love for the flag which waved on the other side of the border and which represented a rivalry contested on many a battlefield. When, therefore, James Stuart, King of Scotland, ascended the throne of England and united the two crowns, there was bound to be bitter dispute with regard to the precedence of the two flags. The Scots held that a Scottish King had become Sovereign of England and that his silver saltire should have the priority. Englishmen maintained that their country was the greater and more important of the two, and infuriated the Scots by hoisting the St. George above the St. Andrew. In order to stop these disputes, the King decided to create a British flag by uniting the two banners. He accordingly issued a proclamation to give effect to this as follows:

"By the King

"Whereas some differences hath arisen between our subjects of South and North Britaine travelling by seas, about the bearing of their Flagges: For the avoiding of all contentions hereafter, Wee have, with the advice of our Councill, ordered: That from henceforth all our Subjects of this Isle and Kingdome of Great Britaine, and all our members thereof, shall beare in their main toppe the Red Crosse, commonly called St. George's Crosse, and the White Crosse, commonly called St. Andrew's Crosse, joyned together according to the forme made by our heralds and sent by Us to our Admerall to be published to our Subjects: and in their fore-toppe our Subjects of South Britaine shall weare the Red Crosse onely as they were wont, and our Subjects of North Britaine in their fore-toppe the White Crosse onely as they were accustomed."

The flag produced by the Heralds was, *Azure, a saltire argent, overall a cross gules fimbriated of the second*. This pleased nobody. The Scots disliked it because their flag was surmounted by the Cross of St. George. The English disliked it because, whereas the St. Andrew's banner was preserved entire, the silver field of their own banner was reduced to a fimbriation. The Navy was annoyed because the King's ships were treated in exactly the same way as the merchantmen. However, the flag, except for the period of the Commonwealth, had come to stay; though in Charles I's reign its use at sea was restricted to the Navy.

After the Union of Ireland with England and Scotland it was a logical development to incorporate the emblem of St. Patrick with that of the other two Saints. No arms had ever been produced for St. Patrick, but he was allotted *Argent, a saltire gules*. These arms already belonged to the well-known Irish family of Fitzgerald, and whether there was any connection between the two has never been stated.

The method adopted to unite the cross of St. Patrick with those of St. George and St. Andrew was ingenious. The blue field of St. Andrew was retained. On this was placed a saltire whose limbs were bisected lengthways, that is, the saltire was itself parted per saltire. The crosses of St. Andrew and St. Patrick were now incorporated by counterchanging the saltire, per saltire argent and gules. In the first and third quarters the silver of St. Andrew was the uppermost part of the limb of the saltire, and in the second and fourth quarters the red of St. Patrick was uppermost. Precedence was given to Scotland as the senior Kingdom of the two by the retention of the blue field, and by the allotment of the most honourable position on the saltire in the senior quarter of the flag. In order that the red saltire should not rest on a blue field it was given a silver fimbriation. Overall was placed the cross of St. George, fimbriated as before. The official blazon now read as follows: *"The Union Flag shall be Azure, the Crosses Saltire of St. Andrew and St. Patrick, Quarterly per saltire counterchanged Argent and Gules, the latter fimbriated of the second, surmounted by the Cross of St. George of the third fimbriated as the Saltire."*

Following the Order in Council and Royal Proclamation creating a new flag, the Admiralty is charged with the responsibility of seeing that it is correctly made up and properly flown. The following table of proportions was accordingly produced for a flag of 15 feet by 7½ feet:

				ft.	in.	
The + of	St George	1/5	together 1/3	1	6	1/3
	Two borders 1/15 each	2/15		1	0	
The × of	St. Patrick	1/15	together 1/10	0	6	1/5
	Its border	1/30		0	3	
	St. Andrew	1/10		0	9	

There are one or two interesting points about these dimensions:

1. The saltire of St. Patrick is made narrower than that of St. Andrew because its fimbriation is taken from itself instead of, as normally, from the field.

2. The fimbriations of St. George and St. Patrick are of different dimensions.

3. The fimbriation of St. George is so wide that, in appearance, it ceases to be a fimbriation and becomes *A cross argent, surmounted by another gules.*

PLATE 17. THE COLOURS OF A REGIMENT OF THE INFANTRY OF THE LINE IN 1751

The Fourth Regiment of Foot now the
King's Own Royal Regiment.
Top: First Colour.
Bottom: Second Colour

The Colours of the Army are the responsibility of the College of Arms, and in these the blazon is strictly adhered to. The fimbriation of St. Patrick is taken from the field, so that the two saltires are of the same width. The fimbriations of St. George and St. Patrick are also of the same width and are both very narrow.

A respect for the laws of armory in the design of national flags is surprisingly widespread. An interesting example is provided by a letter concerning the Battle Flag of the Confederate States of America, possibly the most beautiful flag which has ever been designed. The letter is written by Colonel Wm. Porcher Miles, Chairman of the House Military Committee, C.S.A., and is addressed to General G. T. Beauregard in August 1861.

"In the form I proposed the cross was more heraldic than ecclesiastical, it being the saltire of heraldry. . . . The stars ought always to be white, or argent. . . . Stars, too, show better on an azure field than any other. Blue stars on a white field would not be handsome or appropriate. The white edge to the blue is partly a necessity to prevent what is called false blazoning, or a solecism in heraldry, viz. blazoning colour on colour or metal on metal. It would not do to put a blue cross, therefore, on a red field. Hence the white being metal argent, is put on the red, and the blue put on the white. The introduction of the white between the blue and the red adds also much to the brilliancy of the colours and brings them out in strong relief. But I am boring you with my pet hobby. . . ."

The blazon of this flag is, *Gules, on a saltire azure fimbriated argent, thirteen stars of the last.*

MILITARY FLAGS

The flags of the British Army afford a very interesting study, for in them is enshrined all the usage and traditions of the ensigns of chivalry. We have seen that the basic units of the old mediaeval forces were the bodies of knights and men-at-arms who followed the banner of a knight-banneret or minor baron. These, in turn, formed part of the larger force of one of the great feudal lords. When the feudal forces were replaced by the standing army of the King, companies, each raised by their own captain, replaced the minor units of the private armies and each company fought under the Colour or ensign of its captain. Companies were later formed into regiments, but the Company Colours were still for some time retained in the infantry of the line and still exist in the regiments of foot guards. The Colours which were carried by infantry, when the Regular Army was founded after the Restoration, are described by Captain Thomas Venn, writing in 1672: "The Colonel's colour, in the first place, is of a pure clean colour, without any mixture. The lieutenant-colonel's only with St. George's Armes in the upper corner next the staff; the major's the same, with a little stream blazant, and every captain with St. George's Armes alone, but with so many spots or several devices as pertain to the dignity of their several places." Normally, however, the Cross of St. George occupied the whole field instead of being in a canton and it was usually fimbriated argent.

A very full description of the development of Colours in a regiment of the line is given by Colonel L. I. Cowper, O.B.E., D.L., in his book *The King's Own. The Story of a Royal Regiment.* The first Colours of the King's Own were red with gold rays issuing from each angle of the St. George's Cross. In 1684 the Regiment had become the "Duchess of York and Albany's" and was given new Colours which had a yellow field (the Duke of York's favourite colour). They were described as "a Red Cross in a Yellow Field bordered White with Rays, as that of the Admiral's, with her Royal Highnesses Cypher in the Centre". When the Duke of York ascended the throne as James II the Regiment became the Queen's Regiment and the Colours became the Royal white. The colonel's Colour was white charged with the Queen's cypher in gold ensigned with the crown. The lieutenant-colonel's had the St George's Cross within each quarter five eagles displayed black, beaked and legged gold. The eagle was the crest of the d'Este family, to which the Queen belonged. The major's was the same as the lieutenant-colonel's, but with a red wavy pile issuing from the dexter chief. The eldest captain's was the same as the lieutenant-colonel's, but had the cypher and the crown in the centre. The Colours of the younger captains were probably the same as the eldest captain's but distinguished by numerals.

The Colours of 1702 are described in the Great Wardrobe Accounts:

"One of White Taffaty with the Queen's Cypher painted with gold on both sides and a crowne over each for ye Colonel.

"One other of Crimson and White Taffaty in a Cross, and a Crowne painted on both sides for ye Lieutenant-Colonel.

"One other of Crimson and White Taffaty in a Cross and a blaze of White and a crowne painted on both sides for ye Major.

"Three staves with screwed gilt heads and brass ferruls and a pair of Crimson Tassels with Crimson strings to each of them with Sockets to ye Colours to fix them.

"Nyne colours of White and Crimson Taffaty in a cross, painted on both sides, each Colour distinguished as follows (vizt):

A shaft of Arrows and Crowne
A Pomgranat and Crowne

The Feathers and Crowne
A Star and Crowne
A Wheatsheaf and Crowne
A Beacon and Crowne
A half moone and Crowne
A Bull and Crowne
A Boar and Crowne
Nyne staves with screwed gild heads etc."

In 1707 the above Colours were altered by the addition of the Union Flag. During the reign of Queen Anne the Company Colours disappeared from line regiments, leaving only the colonel's and lieutenant-colonel's. The Colours carried at the Battle of Culloden are still in existence and hang in the Museum at Edinburgh Castle together with the Appin Stewart Colour, at the request of General David Stewart, in order that "the Colours which were opposed to each other at Culloden might thereafter rest in peace side by side". The colonel's Colour is blue charged with crossed sceptres and the crown. The lieutenant-colonel's is the Union charged with crossed sceptres and the Royal Crest.

In 1751 a Royal Warrant introduced new regulations for the Colours of a regiment of the line:

"The King's or 1st Colour of every Regiment is to be the great Union throughout. The 2nd Colour to be the Colour of the facing of the Regiment with the Union in the upper canton: except those Regiments which are faced with red or white whose second Colour is to be the red cross of St. George in a white field and the Union in the Upper canton. In the centre of each Colour is to be painted or embroidered in gold Roman characters the number of the rank of the Regiment within a wreath of roses and thistles on the same stalk except those Regiments which are allowed to wear any Royal devices or ancient badges on whose Colours the rank of the Regiment is to be painted towards the upper corner. The size of the Colour and the length of the pikes to be same as the Royal Regiment of Foot Guards. The cords and tassels of all Colours to be crimson and gold mixed." The size of these Colours was six foot six inches flying and six foot 2 inches on the staff. In accordance with the regulation concerning badges, the King's Own were allowed to bear, "In the centre of their Colours the Kings cypher on a red ground within the Garter and the Crown over it; in the three corners of their 2nd Colour the Lion of England being their ancient badge." Rather oddly the lion passant guardant of England appears on the Colours as crowned. In this Warrant the Regiment is styled the Fourth or the King's Own Royal Regiment and the facing is directed to be blue.

PLATE 18

REGIMENTAL COLOURS

PRE-1858 COLOURS OF THE 6TH OR ROYAL WARWICKSHIRE REGIMENT

These are the large un-fringed colours with the spear head on the colour pike.

PRE-1881 COLOURS OF THE 24TH OR 2ND WARWICKSHIRE REGIMENT, NOW THE
SOUTH WALES BORDERERS

*The silver wreath of immortelles was granted by Queen Victoria to be carried in perpetuity
on the Sovereign's Colour in recognition of the heroism shown by the Regiment at
Isandhlwana and Rorke's Drift in the Zulu War.*

MODERN COLOURS OF THE CHESHIRE REGIMENT

In 1756 the Garter was surrounded by the Union wreath and on the Garter of the second Colour the words "The King's Own Infantry" was substituted for the motto. The Roman iv's and the Lions were also wreathed. In 1801 all regiments were ordered to add the saltire of St. Patrick to the Union and the shamrock to the wreath. After two previous reductions the dimensions of the Colours became fixed in 1868 at three foot nine inches flying and three foot on the pole. In 1858 the Royal Crest of England replaced the spearhead on the staff and the Colours were given a fringe of mixed gold and silk. After the amalgamations of 1881 the Union was removed from the canton of the Regimental Colours. The present Colours are as follows:

1. The Queen's Colour. The Union. In the centre a circle ensigned with the Imperial crown and inscribed "The King's Own Royal Regiment", within which is the word "Lancaster". On the dexter and sinister limbs of the St. George's Cross scrolls bearing battle honours of the war of 1914 to 1918.

2. The Regimental Colour. Blue. In the centre a circle ensigned with the Imperial Crown and surrounded by the Union wreath, inscribed "The King's Own Royal Regiment (Lancaster)", within which is Garter enclosing the Royal cypher on a red ground; the whole surrounded by a laurel wreath charged with scrolls of battle honours prior to 1914; in each of the four corners the lion passant guardant crowned gold.

In the Brigade of Guards the Queen's Colour is always crimson (with the Union in the canton of the Colour of the 2nd and 3rd battalions), and the Regimental Colour is the Union. Both are charged with the battle honours. In addition, each company has a Company Colour and a badge. The badges are borne in rotation in the centre of the Regimental Colour. The Company Colours are square, except for those of the Welsh Guards, which are of the same design as the old standards. The arms of Wales are next to the staff, "Quarterly, or and gules, as many lions passant guardant counterchanged". The remainder is parted per fess argent and vert and charged with two gold dragons and two bendwise bands inscribed with the motto. The flag has a gold ornamental design towards the fly, where it is slit, and is surrounded by a gold and red fringe.

Standards are carried by the Household Cavalry and the regiments of dragoon guards. These are crimson, rectangular in shape and are charged with badges and battle honours in much the same way as Colours. Regiments of dragoons bear guidons, which are also crimson, have rounded corners and are slit at the fly. They too, are charged with badges and battle honours.

The Queen's and Regimental Colours of the Royal Marines are somewhat similar to those of the infantry of the line, except that the Regimental

H   113

Colour follows the old practice of placing the Union in the canton. There are a certain number of Queen's Colours belonging to the Royal Navy for use with Guards of Honour, etc. These consist of the White Ensign (the banner of St. George with the Union in the canton) charged with the Royal cypher within the Garter and ensigned with the Imperial Crown.

THE RIGHT TO FLY FLAGS

The Royal Standard is emblazoned with the Sovereign's personal arms and should never be flown on shore or at sea unless the Sovereign is actually there. Similarly, each of the quarterings of the banner are the arms of the Sovereign for the kingdom which they represent. It would be most improper, therefore, for a private individual to display, for instance, the lion and double tressure of Scotland or the gold harp on a blue field of Ireland. Strangely enough, although the arms for use by the Sovereign in Scotland have Scotland in the first and fourth quarters, England in the second and Ireland in the third, the same Royal Standard as used in England is flown when the Sovereign is present. The Royal Standard of Scotland is hoisted at Holyrood by Royal Command during the residence of the Lord High Commissioner to the General Assembly and upon Royal anniversaries.

The position of the Union Flag, or "Union Jack" as it is commonly called, is peculiar. It is essentially the fighting flag of the Sovereign, and it embodies the emblems of the saints under whose patronage the three kingdoms have fought. Some years ago an official statement was made in Parliament which declared that the Union Jack is the National Flag and may be flown as such on land by any British subject. But no Royal Warrant was ever issued to give effect to this statement; and the College of Arms has recently ruled that the Union Flag is a Royal flag and that, strictly speaking, its use should be confined (on land) to Royal Government property only. Undoubtedly the correct flag for the private individual to fly is the banner of his own personal arms.

Considerable doubt seems to exist as to the correct flag to be flown from church towers. As regards the Church of England, it was laid down by the College of Arms in 1930, at the request of the Archbishops of Canterbury and York, that the proper flag to be flown from churches is the flag of St. George with a shield of the arms of the diocese in the first quarter. A similar arrangement would seem to be a very suitable one for the Roman Catholic Church, if the position as regards its diocesan arms could be regularised. In the meantime Catholic churches, and those of other denominations, could presumably fly the banner of the patron saint of the realm or of the particular church.

Chapter XIII

ROYAL HERALDRY

THE Royal Arms of England are nearly as old as heraldry, for they first appear on the second Great Seal of King Richard I. Several theories have been produced to account for the origin of these arms, but there is little evidence to support them. Henry I may, however, have used a lion as a charge or a badge, as the offspring of his illegitimate sons bore lions, and he presented a shield charged with rampant lions to his son-in-law Geoffrey of Anjou. Prince John, before he succeeded his brother as King, bore *Gules, two lions passant in pale or*. King Richard I's first Great Seal shows the dexter half of his shield charged with one lion rampant to the sinister, and it is likely that a similar lion rampant to the dexter was charged on the hidden sinister half. It appears, therefore, to have been a family habit to bear lions and that the present arms of *Gules, three lions passant guardant in pale or*, were King Richard's second choice. That they became permanent may be due to the prestige and glory they acquired from their feared and famous bearer.

Many writers have asserted that the lions in the Royal Arms are really leopards, but it seems clear from the family taste for lions that King Richard never intended to represent any other beast. Nevertheless, the lions in the English coat were more generally referred to as leopards for the first two centuries of their existence. Three leopards were sent as a present to King Henry III by the Emperor Frederick II in reference to his arms, and in the reign of King Henry V there was a Leopard Herald. In the early days of heraldry, however, a leopard was not known except by repute, and his most noted characteristic was his quiet cat-like walk as compared with the noisy and aggressive habits of the lion. The normal position of a lion was therefore supposed to be rampant. In the passant guardant attitude a lion was held to be behaving like a leopard, and was therefore so called. The blazon *"Gules, three leopards in pale or"* was therefore an adequate description of the English arms, since the name of the beast gave the attitude. In French blazon these old rules are still observed. A *lion* is a lion rampant and a *léopard* is a lion passant guardant. In addition there are descriptions of attitudes between these two. A *lion-léopardé* is a lion passant, that is a lion looking to its front like a lion but walking like a leopard. Similarly a *léopard-lionné* is a lion rampant guardant.

The Royal Arms remained unchanged until, in 1340, King Edward III quartered them with the Arms of France, to emphasise his claim to the French throne. The Royal Arms of France, *Azure, semé-de-lis or*, were placed in the first and fourth quarters and those of England in the second and third. (These early French arms are known as "France ancient" to distinguish them from the later modification of *Azure, three fleurs-de-lis or*, which is called "France modern".) The fleur-de-lis was used as a decoration long before the days of heraldry, and it appears as an ornament on sceptre and crown in the fifth century. The theories as to its origin are numerous, but it is now most generally considered to be a representation of the iris flower, which until recent years was known as a lily. The popular French legend states that a lily was brought from Heaven by an angel to Clovis, King of the Franks, on the occasion of his baptism as a special mark of Our Lady's favour. The lily has, of course, always been the especial symbol of Our Lady.

King Richard II impaled the quartered arms of France and England with the arms which had been posthumously allotted to the Saint-King, Edward the Confessor. The Confessor's arms were placed on the dexter and those of England and France on the sinister. St. Edward's arms were *Azure, a cross patonce between five martlets or*. These arms are supposed to have been derived from the doves which appear on the coins of the Confessor's reign.

In 1376 Charles V of France reduced the number of fleurs-de-lis in his arms to three "pour symboliser la Sainte-Trinité". This arrangement had, in fact, been used occasionally as early as 1280. In 1405 King Henry IV followed suit, and in 1411 he put these altered arms on his own Great Seal.

On the marriage of Queen Mary I with King Philip II of Spain the quartered arms of France and England were impaled with those of Spain, and the impaled arms of the two kingdoms are shown on her second Great Seal.

In Queen Elizabeth I's reign the arms of Ireland, *Azure, a harp, or, stringed argent*, made their first appearance in the third quarter of the Royal shield; but they were not always included. The harp is an ancient Irish symbol, but it was first used as a Royal badge on the Irish coins of King Henry VIII, surmounted by a crown. The arms previously associated with Ireland were the three gold crowns on a blue field, assigned to St. Edmund, which are at present the arms of the province of Munster, and three crowns appear on Edward IV's Irish half-groat. It was possibly under the banner of St. Edmund that Richard of Clare, Earl of Pembroke, known as Strongbow, invaded Ireland in 1170. They are also the arms of Sweden, and it was probably from that country that they came originally.

In the eyes of all Catholics, of course, Elizabeth I was illegitimate and therefore usurping the throne. By legitimate descent, from the eldest daughter of King Henry VII, Mary Queen of Scots was considered to be the real Sovereign of England. The successive arms borne by Mary Queen of Scots are interesting. Her maiden arms had Scotland in the first and fourth quarters and France modern quartered with England in the second and third. After her marriage with the Dauphin of France the combined coat showed the arms of the Dauphin (France modern quartered with the Dauphiné, *Or, a dolphin embowed azure, finned and langued gules*) in the first and fourth quarters and those of Scotland in the second and third. On an inescutcheon of pretence was the quartered shield of France and England to show his wife's pretensions to the throne of England. The bearing of such an inescutcheon by the Dauphin is of peculiar interest. The quartering of the arms of France in the English Royal achievement signified the claim of English Sovereigns to the throne of France. Heraldically the Dauphin, heir himself to the French throne, was admitting this claim but maintaining that his own wife was the heir to the thrones of France and England! After the death of the Dauphin, Queen Mary dimidiated her husband's quartered coat, including the inescutcheon, and placed it on the dexter side of her shield. On the sinister side she put her own undimidiated maiden arms. It was really a reversion to the early system of marshalling arms already mentioned by which the more important arms appeared to overlap the less important.

The Royal Arms of Scotland are *Or, a lion rampant within a double tressure flory-counter-flory gules*. A rampant lion first appears on the Great Seal of King Alexander II (1214-89) and there appear to be traces of what may have been a tressure or bordure. It is likely that the lion, at any rate, was borne by King William the Lion (1165-1214), who may have been so named from his cognisance. On the first Great Seal of Alexander III (1249-86) the shield of the equestrian figure of the King appears to bear the lion alone, but on the bardings of the horse the lion is surrounded by a bordure charged with cross crosslets and having demi fleurs-de-lis on the inner edge. The double tressure as we know it to-day was certainly in use before the end of the reign of Alexander III. It is traditionally supposed to have owed its origin to the guardianship of Scotland by France, but there is no evidence to support this, and it may have developed from an ornamental structural band round the edge of the shield. Nevertheless, the tradition that in some way the tressure indicated subordination to France seems to have been held at an early date, for about 1471 the Scots Parliament advised King James III to remove the tressure from his arms. At that time the King was contemplating a visit to the French court. There is no evidence that this advice was ever acted upon, though in some representations of the arms at this period the part of the tressure above the lion was omitted; perhaps to show friendship and alliance with France but to deny any suggestion of her overlordship. The tressure cannot now be granted to anyone without the express licence of the Sovereign, though this does not prevent it being borne by anyone who can prove descent from an ancestor entitled to it.

After the union of the two crowns under King James VI of Scotland and I of England there were two arrangements of the Royal Arms. In England the quartered coat of France and England was placed in the first and fourth quarters, Scotland in the second and Ireland in the third. In Scotland the Scottish Royal Arms were in the first and fourth quarters, those of France and England in the second and the harp of Ireland in the third.

The Commonwealth produced some extraordinary arms after the execution of Charles I. The Cross of St. George was placed in the first and fourth quarters, the saltire of St. Andrew in the second, whilst the arms of Ireland were retained unaltered in the third quarter. Overall on an inescutcheon of pretence were the personal arms of Cromwell, *Sable, a lion rampant argent.*

King Charles II resumed the arms of his father and grandfather. The next change took place after the Revolution and the accession of William III and Mary II. The shield was impaled, with the previous Royal Arms on both the dexter and sinister sides, to show the equal sovereignty of the two monarchs. Over the arms on the dexter side William III placed the arms of Nassau, *Azure, billettée a lion rampant or,* on an inescutcheon of pretence to show that he was an elected monarch. After the death of Mary, the impaled coat was discontinued and William III used the Stuart Royal Arms with the inescutcheon of Nassau.

When Queen Anne succeeded to the throne she adopted the same arms but dropped the inescutcheon of Nassau. The Royal Arms were thus once again those borne by King James I. After the Act of Union with Scotland in 1707 there was a further change. France disappeared from the first and fourth quarters and the old quartered English arms were replaced by England impaled with Scotland. France was placed in the second quarter and Ireland, as before, in the third. In England the English arms were on the dexter side of the impalement and the Scottish on the sinister. In Scotland this arrangement was reversed. In this impalement the tressure was dimidiated.

On the accession of King George I the arms of Hanover were included in the Royal achievement. These were, *Tierced in pairle reversed, dexter, Gules, two lions passant guardant in pale or (for Brunswick):*

*sinister, Or, semé of hearts gules, a lion rampant azure (for Luneberg):
in base, Gules, a horse courant argent (for Westphalia): overall an inescutcheon of pretence, Gules, the Crown of Charlemagne or.* The Hanoverian
arms replaced the unpaled arms of England and Scotland in the fourth
quarter. The resulting coat could still be seen at the head of *The Times*
newspaper until 1953.

In 1801, following the Union of Great Britain and Ireland, the arms
of France were removed from the Royal Arms in order that the arms of
the three United Kingdoms could be shown equally. The arms of England.
were placed in the first and fourth quarters, those of Scotland on the
second quarter and the harp of Ireland in the third quarter. (The precedence of the English and Scottish arms were reversed in Scotland.)
The arms of Hanover appeared in an inescutcheon of pretence which
was surmounted by an Electoral bonnet. In 1816 Hanover became a
Kingdom and the Electoral bonnet was replaced by a foreign Royal
crown.

When Queen Victoria acceded to the throne in 1837 the Kingdom
of Hanover, owing to the Salic law, ceased to be associated with the
United Kingdom, and the Hanoverian arms disappeared from the Royal
shield. The quartered arms of England, Scotland and Ireland remained
as they are displayed in the Royal achievement to-day.

In Scotland precedence is normally given to the Scottish arms, but
this practice has not been universal. It is, however, correct and it has
the authority of the Treaty of Union. As has already been mentioned,
however, when the Sovereign is in residence in Scotland the Royal
Standard displays the Scottish arms in the second quarter.

The Royal Crest of England is *"Upon the Royal Helm the Imperial
Crown proper, supporting a lion statant guardant or, imperially crowned
also proper"*. A lion appears on the headdress of Geoffrey of Anjou, and
the second seal of King Richard I shows a lion painted on his helmet.
In both these cases the lion appears to have been taken from the arms
and adapted to the shape of the headgear. The first Royal Crest to be
modelled and placed on top of the helm was an uncrowned statant lion.
There is an excellent example in the helm of the Black Prince which hangs
above his tomb in Canterbury Catherdal. The lion is modelled in cuirbouilli faced with gesso and stands on a chapeau. Later, when crests
had become purely decorative, the statant lion developed into the lion
statant guardant and crowned.

The Scottish Royal Crest first appeared on the helm of King Robert II
in 1370. The Armorial de Gelre shows the lion as sejant, crowned and
holding a sword. On the seal, however, the crest is a lion statant guardant.
This seal version was continued until the death of King James V, though

sometimes the lion was shown as statant only. The sejant lion was used in the Royal achievement, however, and became the lion sejant erect affronté, which is the Scottish Royal Crest of to-day.

The Royal Crest of Ireland is a white hart springing from a triple-turreted tower. This crest originated from King Richard II's expedition to Ireland. The white hart was his favourite badge.

The use of supporters with the English Royal Arms really started in the reign of King Richard II; though King Edward III sometimes used a golden lion and a silver falcon. Richard II's first supporters were two angels, one on each side of the shield, and below the shield a white hart couchant, gorged and chained gold under a tree. Later he adopted two white harts. Henry IV at first used two white swans adapted from the de Bohun badge, each holding an ostrich feather in his bill. These were later replaced by a white swan on the dexter side and an antelope on the sinister. Finally Henry IV changed to a gold rampant lion on the dexter side and a white antelope on the sinister. King Henry V kept the same supporters. King Henry VI's first supporters were two antelopes. (The antelope was also a de Bohun badge.) These were succeeded by a lion and antelope and then by a lion and an heraldic tyger. King Edward IV had the silver rampant lion of March on the dexter side with its tail passed between its legs and over its back.

The sinister supporter varied between a white hart, a gold lion, a silver lion and the black bull of Clare. Richard III's supporters were his favourite white boars, with gold tusks and bristles. The dexter boar was occasionally replaced by a gold lion. Three different varieties of supporters were used by King Henry VII: a red dragon and a silver greyhound, a lion and a dragon, and two silver greyhounds. King Henry VIII used more different supporters than any other Sovereign. A golden lion was combined with, in turn, a red dragon, an heraldic antelope, a silver bull and a cock. Other varieties were an heraldic antelope and stag, a dragon and greyhound, and two greyhounds. Edward VI used a gold lion with either a red dragon or a silver greyhound. Queen Mary I's supporters were the same before her marriage, except that the dragon was gold. After her marriage with King Philip the Imperial eagle appeared as the dexter supporter with a gold crowned lion on the sinister. Elizabeth I reverted to some of the supporters used by her father; a gold lion and a red dragon, a red dragon and a silver greyhound, and an heraldic antelope and a stag.

King James I brought the unicorn with him to the English throne and was the first monarch to use the supporters that uphold the Royal shield at the present time. A single unicorn appears first as a supporter on a coin of James I of Scotland, and the single unicorn was never

PLATE 19

A DESIGN FOR THE ROYAL ARMS

entirely abandoned until the reign of James VI, though the shields of James III and succeeding Sovereigns were frequently supported by two unicorns. On the Scottish Privy Seal two lions supported the shield up till the union of the two crowns. Queen Mary, for instance, had unicorns on her Great Seal and lions on her Privy Seal. In one representation of James I's supporters the lion holds a banner charged with a cross patonce and the unicorn a banner of the arms of St. Edward the Confessor. Although the lion and the unicorn had come to stay in the Royal achievement, many of the Sovereigns up till the time of George I occasionally used other supporters as well. A griffin and a greyhound appear in the reigns of James I, Charles II, and George I. Charles I had a heraldic antelope and a stag, and a dragon and heraldic antelope. James II had two greyhounds each holding an ostrich feather. Anne used a lion and a greyhound.

In the Royal achievement for use in Scotland the unicorn is on the dexter side of the shield holding the banner of St. Andrew, whilst the lion is on the sinister and holds the banner of St. George. The shield in the Scottish Royal Arms is supported by two unicorns, of which the dexter holds the Scottish Royal banner, and the sinister, St. Andrew's banner.

Since the reign of Queen Elizabeth I, the mantling in the Royal achievement has been gold-lined ermine. Previous to that it was gules lined ermine. The compartment includes the rose, thistle and shamrock growing from the same stem. In the Scottish version of the Royal Arms, however, the thistle only is generally shown. The arms of a Queen consort are the Royal Arms impaled with her own paternal arms. In the case of Queen Elizabeth, the Queen Mother, these were (and are): *Quarterly,* 1st and 4th, *Argent, a lion rampant within a double tressure flory-counter-flory azure;* 2nd and 3rd, *Ermine, three bows palewise in fess proper.*

The Royal Arms are differenced in an entirely different way to those of the Queen's subjects. The Royal Arms are not, of course, personal to the Monarch. They are the sovereign arms of dominion and may only be borne undifferenced by the actual occupant of the throne. Originally the Royal Arms were differenced either by a bordure or a label. The label first employed for the Heir Apparent was azure. When, however, the arms of France were quartered with those of England, the use of an azure label was no longer possible, and the Heir Apparent has been distinguished ever since by a plain white label of three points. At the same time labels used for other members of the Royal Family were altered to white, but in their case the points of the labels were charged with various objects, which were frequently taken from the arms of a female ancestor. This is the method now always used for members of the Royal Family. The labels may have either three or five points, and the points bear such charges as anchors, roses, crosses, fleurs-de-lis, thistles and hearts. The use of the bordure was discontinued in the Tudor era.

The motto of the King of England was originally "God and my right shall me defend". This was shortened to "God and my right" or "Dieu et mon droit"; and in this form it was probably used to signify the claim to the French throne. "Dieu et mon droit" appears on a motto scroll below the present Royal achievement. The ancient motto of the Kings of Scotland was "In my defence God me defend". This was abbreviated to "In Defens", and is placed above the crest in the Royal Arms as used in Scotland.

Chapter XIV

KNIGHTHOOD

IN the Middle Ages a knight bore his insignia about his person. These were his golden spurs, his lance and pennon, his sword, his shield of arms and his belt. Of these the sword and belt have lasted through the ages to the armed forces of the King to-day, and have retained some of their original traditions. Of the belt, Guillim says, "And not without reason is a man adorned with a Military girdle, signifying he must be always in readiness to undergo the business of the Weal Publick; for the more speedy performance of which charge, he should have his Garments close girt unto his body, that the looseness of these should give no impediment to the execution of his assumed charge and enjoyned Services." And, "As the bestowing of this Military Girdle was reputed very honourable, because none were to receive it but men of merit, so also was it ever accounted most dishonourable for any just cause to be again deprived of the Dignity thereof." Knights-banneret, as has already been stated, carried a banner of their arms instead of a knight's pennon.

The last knight-banneret to be created on the field of battle was Major-General John Ligonier, at Dettingen, by King George II. He was also, probably, the last legitimate one since knights-banneret could, in fact, only be created on the battlefield. The ordinary knight still exists as a "knight bachelor". His armorial achievement is distinguished by his knight's helm, and in 1926 King George V sanctioned the use of a gold and red enamel badge to be worn on the left breast. The badge incorporates in its design the knight's belt, sword and spurs.

In about 1347-49 King Edward III instituted the Most Noble Order of the Garter, the first and the most eminent of the British orders of knighthood. Its origin is unknown. According to popular legend the Countess of Warwick dropped one of her garters on the floor at a Court function, and the King, to cover her embarrassment, picked it up and put it on his own leg, saying, "Shame be to him who thinks ill of it." Froissart, however, connects the foundation of the order with a revival by the King of King Arthur's Knights of the Round Table, known as the Knights of the Blue Garter, with an annual feast on St. George's Day. The best-known part of the insignia is, naturally, the blue velvet garter. This is inscribed in gold letters with the motto of the order, *"Honi Soit qui mal y pense"*, and is worn by knights below the left knee with the end looped in the distinctive garter fashion. Ladies of the order wear it above the left elbow. The collar of the order is of gold and consists of twenty-six garters (representing the Sovereign and twenty-five knight companions) each encircling a rose and alternating with gold knots. From the collar is suspended the "George", an enamel figure of St. George on a white horse slaying the dragon. The collar is worn on "Collar Days" with a mantle of dark blue velvet, lined with taffeta and charged on the left shoulder with a garter enclosing a shield of the arms of St. George. (The Sovereign has the star of the order embroidered on the mantle instead of this device.) With the mantle are worn a crimson hood, and a black velvet hat ornamented with a plume of white ostrich feathers, in the centre of which is a tuft of black heron's feathers.

The other insignia of the order are the star and the riband, neither of which are worn with the collar. The star is silver, has eight rays and is charged with the garter encircling the Cross of St. George. It was devised in the second year of King Charles I by surrounding the badge with rays of silver. It is worn on the left breast. The riband is blue (the shade of blue is changed for each Sovereign) and is worn across the body from the left shoulder to the right hip. Suspended from the riband over the hip is the "Lesser George", a gold badge of St. George and the dragon encircled by the garter. A Knight of the Garter encircles his shield with the garter. Outside this he may place the collar of the order, but the garter may be borne alone, and, in fact, generally is on representations of the Royal Arms. A Knight of the Garter is entitled to claim a grant of supporters, if he does not already possess them.

The second order of knighthood in importance is the Most Ancient and Most Noble Order of the Thistle. It probably has as early an origin as the Order of the Garter, since the figure of St. Andrew bearing his saltire in front of him, which is now the badge of the order, appears on the reverse of the coins of King Robert II (1370-90). Tradition assigns its institution to a far more remote period.

In the sixteenth century the order fell into disuse, but it was revived by King James II of England in 1687 and was re-established by a statute passed in the reign of Queen Anne. The collar is formed of sixteen thistles, in allusion to the number of knights of the order, alternating with sprigs of rue. To the collar is attached the pendant, which is a golden star of eight rays charged with the figure of St. Andrew, habited in a green mantle and purple surcoat and bearing his white saltire before him. The mantle is of green velvet lined with taffeta tied with tasselled cords of green and gold and charged with the representation of the star of the order on the left shoulder. The hat is of black velvet ornamented with white osprey plumes. The star is a saltire of silver with rays issuing from its angles, and charged with a thistle on a gold field surrounded by a green circlet of the order inscribed *"Nemo me impure lacessit"* ("No one touches me with impunity"). The riband is dark green and worn over the left shoulder. Suspended from it over the right hip is the jewel, which is enamelled gold with on the obverse St. Andrew and his saltire and on the reverse the thistle, all in proper colours; the whole surrounded by an oval inscribed with the motto. A Knight of the Thistle may surround his arms with the circlet and the collar of the order and may obtain a grant of supporters. The Royal Arms for use in Scotland and the Royal Arms of Scotland are generally surrounded by the collar only, which is the opposite of the practice adopted with the Garter.

The senior Irish order is the Most Illustrious Order of St. Patrick. It is much more recent than the two former since it was instituted by King George III in 1783. The collar is composed of roses alternating with harps and tied together with knots of gold. The roses are alternately red petals upon white and white petals upon red, and are each surrounded by a bordure charged with shamrocks.

In the centre of the collar is a harp surmounted by an Imperial Crown, from which hangs the badge. The badge is oval in shape and consists of the saltire of St. Patrick charged with a shamrock slipped and bearing an Imperial Crown on each leaf, the whole surrounded by the sky-blue circlet of the order inscribed *"Quis separatit MDCCLXXXIII"*, within another circlet of gold charged with green shamrocks. The mantle is of sky-blue Irish poplin lined with white silk, fastened by a cord of gold and blue silk and charged on the right side with a representation of the star of the order. The hat is of black velvet with a representation of the star fixed to the front. The riband is sky blue and worn over the right shoulder. When the riband is worn the badge is detached from the collar and is suspended from the riband over the left hip. The star is silver with eight rays. In the centre is the circlet, enclosing the same design as on the badge. Knights of St. Patrick may surround their arms with the circlet and collar of the order. They also may claim a grant of supporters.

Replicas of the stars of these three orders are worn as cap badges by three of the regiments of foot guards. The Star of the Garter is worn by the Coldstream Guards, the Star of the Thistle by the Scots Guards and the Star of St. Patrick by the Irish Guards.

The Most Honourable Order of the Bath is another very ancient order. It was originally founded in 1399, but subsequently fell into disuse. It was revived by King George I in 1725. Its name is derived from the ceremonial bathing which was observed at a knight's installation. This custom has long since been discontinued. There was originally only one grade in the order, and knights used the abbreviation K.B., but in 1815, after the end of the Napoleonic wars, there were so many whose military services deserved recognition that it was decided to divide the order into three grades or classes. These classes were known as the "Knights Grand Cross" (G.C.B.), the "Knights Commanders" (K.C.B.) and the "Knights Companions" (C.B.). This last does not carry knighthood and is now, in practice, abbreviated to "Companions". The order is divided into a Military and a Civil division.

The insignia of a Knight Grand Cross includes a crimson mantle with a representation of the star of the order on the shoulder, a hat of crimson velvet with a plume of white feathers at the side and a collar of nine golden Imperial Crowns alternating with eight devices of united rose, thistle and shamrock issuing from a sceptre. From one of the crowns hangs the badge, which differs in pattern for the Military and Civil divisions. The Military badge is a white enamelled gold Maltese cross having a gold ball at each point of the cross and a gold Lion of England in each of the angles of the limbs. The cross is charged in the centre with a device of the united rose, thistle and shamrock surmounted by a sceptre in pale between three Imperial Crowns, within a red circlet inscribed *"Tria juncta in uno"*, the whole surrounded by a laurel wreath. On the lower limb is a blue motto scroll inscribed *"Ich dien"*. The Civil badge is all gold and is an enlargement of the same device which is in the centre of the Military badge, surrounded by an oval band inscribed *"Tria juncta in uno"*.

The riband of the order is crimson and is worn over the right shoulder with the badge, which is detached from the collar, resting on the left hip. The Military star is composed of curved rays of silver, surmounted by a gold Maltese cross charged in the centre with three crowns, within a circlet inscribed *"Tria juncta in uno"*, surrounded by a laurel wreath. On the lower limb of the cross is a motto scroll inscribed *"Ich dien"*. A representation of this star is a badge of rank worn by officers of the Army. The Civil star is similar, but does not bear the Maltese cross, laurel wreath or motto "Ich Dien". A Knight Commander has a star and a badge. The Military star is in the form of a silver cross pateé with a small ray at each angle. The device in the centre is the same as that for the G.C.B. The star of the Civil division is similar, but the device in the centre is the same as that for a Civil Knight Grand Cross. The badge for each division is the same as that worn by the Knights Grand Cross, and is suspended at the throat from a crimson riband which passes round the neck. The Companions have the same badge worn in the same way, but no star.

In early times the Knights of the Bath (K.B.) appear to have surrounded their arms with the circlet of the order but not with the collar. A Knight Grand Cross now surrounds his arms with both circlet and collar. If he belongs to the Military division he encircles his arms with the laurel wreath as well, which is placed between the circlet and the collar. Knights Grand Cross are the only class of the order who can claim a grant of supporters. Knights Commanders and Companions surround their arms with the circlet and suspend the badge below the shield from the ribbon with which it is worn. The laurel wreath is placed outside the circlet by Knights Commanders of the Military division.

The Most Exalted Order of the Star of India is the next senior. It was founded by Queen Victoria on 23rd February 1861 and consists of three classes: Knights Grand Commanders (G.C.S.I.), Knights Commanders (K.C.S.I.) and Companions (C.S.I.). Knights Grand Commanders wear a mantle of light blue satin which is lined with white, fastened with a white silk cordon with silver and light-blue tassels and embroidered on the left side with a representation of the star of the order. The collar is composed of lotus flowers, palm branches in saltire and united red and white roses. In the centre is an Imperial Crown, from which is suspended the badge. The badge consists of an onyx cameo bearing a profile bust of Queen Victoria encircled with a blue enamelled band fimbriated with diamonds and inscribed *"Heaven's light our guide"*, the whole surmounted by a mullet set with diamonds. The star is circular of alternate long and short wavy rays of gold, charged with a mullet of diamonds within a blue circlet inscribed, *"Heaven's light our guide"*. The riband is light blue fimbriated white and worn over the right shoulder. The badge is suspended from it over the left hip. A Knight Commander has a similar star, but the rays and mullet are silver. The badge is the same and is worn at the throat suspended from a riband round the neck. A Companion's badge differs from the others in having a mullet of chipped silver. It is also worn at the throat. A G.C.S.I. surrounds his arms with the circlet and the collar, a K.C.S.I. and C.S.I. use the circlet and badge in the same fashion as equivalent grades in the Order of the Bath. A G.C.S.I. may obtain supporters.

The Most Distinguished Order of Saint Michael and Saint George was instituted in 1818 by George IV, whilst Prince Regent, for the purpose of affording a special decoration to the inhabitants of Malta and the Ionian Islands, shortly after the cession of these territories to Great Britain. It is generally now conferred on members of the Diplomatic and Colonial Services, though it was awarded to a number of soldiers for distinguished service in the field during the First World War. It is divided into three classes: Knights Grand Cross (G.C.M.G.), Knights Commanders (K.C.M.G.) and Companions (C.M.G.). The mantle worn by the G.C.M.G. is Saxon-blue satin lined with scarlet silk and tied with a gold, scarlet and blue cordon. On the left side is a representation of the star of the order. The collar is of gold and composed of Lions of England imperially crowned, Maltese crosses and the cyphers "S.M." and "S.G." (in reference to the patron saints of the order) arranged alternately. In the centre is an Imperial Crown over two winged lions passant guardant imperially crowned, each supporting a book and seven arrows. The badge hangs from a clasp beneath the books and consists of a cross of seven double-pointed limbs ensigned with the Imperial Crown and charged in the centre with St. George and the dragon within a blue circlet inscribed *"Auspicium melioris aevi"* ("A pledge for better times").

The same badge is worn by the K.C.M.G. and the C.M.G. The riband is Saxon-blue with a central scarlet stripe and is worn over the right shoulder. The badge is suspended from it over the left hip. The star consists of seven silver rays with a golden ray between each of them. Overall is the Cross of St. George in red enamel charged in the centre with a representation of the Archangel St. Michael within the circlet of the order. The Knight Commander's star has four silver rays charged with a double-pointed saltire, on which is a similar cross and centre as on the Star of a Knight Grand Cross. Both the Knight Commander and the Companion wear the badge suspended from a riband round the neck. The rules for the display of the insignia with arms are the same as for the previous orders, and a G.C.M.G. may similarly obtain a grant of supporters.

The second order awarded for service in or for India is the Most Eminent Order of the Indian Empire, which was founded by Queen Victoria in 1877. It has three classes: Knights Grand Commanders (G.C.I.E.), Knights Commanders (K.C.I.E.) and Companions (C.I.E.). The mantle worn by a Knight Grand Commander is of imperial purple satin, lined with white silk, fastened with a white silk cordon having gold and purple silk tassels and embroidered on the left shoulder with a representation of a G.C.I.E.'s star. The collar is composed of elephants, lotus flowers, peacocks and Indian roses. The badge is suspended from an Imperial Crown and consists of an Indian rose charged in the centre with the profile bust of Queen Victoria within a blue circlet inscribed *"Imperatricis Auspiciis"*. The star of a G.C.I.E. has ten points of which the rays are alternately plain and scaled, five sets of gold rays alternate with five sets of silver rays. In the centre is an effigy of Queen Victoria within the circlet of the order. The riband is dark blue and is worn over the right shoulder with the badge suspended from it over the left hip. The Star of the Knight Commander is the same as that of the Knight Grand Commander except that it is all silver. K.C.I.E.'s and C.I.E.'s wear the badge suspended from the neck. Insignia are displayed with the arms as in the previous orders and a G.C.I.E. may obtain supporters.

The Royal Victorian Order was founded by Queen Victoria in 1896.

Unlike the orders previously considered, it has five classes: Knights Grand Cross (G.C.V.O.), Knights Commanders (K.C.V.O.), Commanders (C.V.O.), Members 4th Class (M.V.O.) and Members 5th Class (M.V.O.). The mantle of the Knight Grand Cross is of dark blue satin edged with red satin and lined with white silk. It is tied with tasselled cordons of gold and dark blue silk. On the left side is embroidered a representation of the G.C.V.O.'s star. The collar consists of gold octagonal pieces, each jewelled with a carbuncle, alternating with gold ornamental frames. The frames are each inscribed with a portion of the legend, "Victoria Britt. Reg. Def. Fid. Ind. Imp." In the centre of the collar is a blue octagonal piece edged with red, in a gold frame and charged with a white saltire on which is a gold medallion of Queen Victoria's effigy. From this piece hangs the badge; a white Maltese cross charged with the cypher V.I.R. on a red field within a blue circlet inscribed "Victoria" and ensigned with the Imperial Crown. The riband is dark blue with a red edging which has a narrow white stripe in its centre. It is worn over the right shoulder and suspends the badge at the left hip.

The star of a Knight Grand Cross is of chipped silver, has eight points and is charged in the centre with a representation of the badge of the order. The Knight Commander's star is a Maltese cross of chipped silver rays with smaller rays issuing from the angles. In the centre is a representation of the badge of the order but with the limbs of the cross in frosted silver instead of white enamel. The K.C.V.O. and C.V.O. wear the badge at the throat suspended from a riband round the neck. Members of the 4th and 5th classes wear the badge on the left breast like a medal. The badge of a M.V.O. 4th Class differs from the others in having a frosted silver, instead of white enamel, cross. In addition to these classes there is a medal of the order known as the "Royal Victorian Medal." It is circular in shape and is worn on the left breast suspended by the riband of the order. The insignia of the three senior classes are displayed with the arms in the same way as in the previous orders. The M.V.O.'s suspend their badge below their arms on a ribbon as it would be worn on the breast. G.C.V.O.'s may claim supporters.

The most junior and most recent of the British orders of knighthood is the Most Excellent Order of the British Empire. It was instituted in 1917 by King George V. There are two divisions—Military and Civil— and five classes; and it may be awarded to both men and women. The classes are: Knights Grand Cross and Dames Grand Cross (G.B.E.), Knights Commanders (K.B.E.) and Dames Commanders (D.B.E.), Commanders (C.B.E.), Officers (O.B.E.) and Members (M.B.E.). The collar is of gold and consists of medallions alternating with two heraldic sea-lions holding tridents, addorsed and reguardant. The medallions bear alternately a shield of the Royal Arms and the cipher G.R.I. The badge, which is suspended from the collar, is a cross patonce of pearl grey enamel edged with gold, ensigned with the Imperial Crown and charged in the centre with the crowned heads of King George V and Queen Mary within a red circlet inscribed, "For God and the Empire". The star of a G.B.E. is silver with eight rays and bears the same device as the badge.

When originally instituted the badge and stars bore the figure of Britannia instead of the heads of the King and Queen. The riband was originally purple with a crimson stripe in the centre for the Military division and purple alone for the Civil division. It is now rose pink with a pearl grey edging and a pearl grey central stripe for the Military division. The riband of the Civil division omits the central stripe. The riband is worn over the right shoulder and the badge is suspended on the left hip. The star of a K.B.E. and a D.B.E. is a cross of four rays with four lesser rays issuing from the angles. It is charged with the same device as the badge and the star of a G.B.E. Dames Grand Cross and Dames have smaller stars than those worn by the men, and the collar of a Dame Grand Cross is smaller and daintier than that of a Knight Grand Cross. K.B.E.'s wear the badge at the throat from a riband which is passed round the neck. D.B.E.'s wear it from a knot of the riband pinned to the left shoulder.

In the case of Commanders the badge is worn by men in the same way as a K.B.E. and by women in the same fashion as a D.B.E. The badge of an Officer is of plain silver gilt and of a Member of plain silver. They are both worn on the left breast like a medal. In addition to these five classes there is a British Empire Medal (B.E.M.), which is worn on the left breast suspended from a riband which has or has not the central stripe according to whether it is a Military or Civil award. The rules for the display of the insignia of the five classes with arms are the same as those for the Royal Victorian Order. But Dames and women Commanders suspend their badge from a bow of the riband. G.B.E.'s are entitled to supporters.

Members of other orders which do not confer the dignity of knighthood and which are of one class only, and holders of decorations, suspend their badge below their shield of arms as it is worn, i.e. from a double ribbon if round the neck or a single ribbon if on the breast. A baronetcy is a form of hereditary knighthood. This dignity was originally instituted by King James I in 1611 as part of his plan for the "plantation" or armed settlement of the Province of Ulster in Ireland. James I, ever careful of the pennies, hit on a brilliant idea which would not only provide him with an army of occupation for nothing, but which would actually enrich the Treasury. He directed that the hereditary title of baronet should be conferred on every gentleman who possessed an estate of the annual value of one thousand pounds and who would undertake to maintain thirty soldiers in Ulster for three years.

The rate of pay was to be eightpence per day per man and "the wages of one whole year to be paid into our receipt upon passing of the patent"! The decree added, "His Majesty doth also grant for him, his heirs, and successors that the baronets, and their descendants, shall, and may bear, either in a canton, in their coat of arms, or in an escutcheon, at their election, the arms of Ulster, that is, in a Field, Argent, a Hand, Gules, or a bloody Hand." Now the peculiar thing about the wording of this paragraph is that the Hand of Ulster, the Red Hand of the O'Neills, is a dexter hand, whereas the hand that is commonly borne by the baronets is sinister. From which some authorities have argued that the baronet's hand is nothing to do with Ulster. However, it is quite clear from the wording of the decree that the Hand of Ulster is intended, and the display of the sinister hand may have been due to some original error.

These baronets were termed "Baronets of England". In 1619 the King founded a new order of "Baronets of Ireland". This was similar to the former except that the fees were paid into the Treasury of Ireland.

The plan for the plantation of Ulster having worked so well and profitably, the King was desirous of founding a similar order for Scotland, to improve the Province of Nova Scotia. He died before he could carry the plan into effect, but the Baronets of Nova Scotia were instituted in 1625 by King Charles I. The King decreed that they should be distinguished by a jewel charged with the arms of the province, *Argent, a saltire azure, on an inescutcheon the Arms of Scotland; above the shield an Imperial Crown. Supporters. Dexter, the Royal Unicorn, sinister, a savage proper. Crest, A laurel branch and a thistle issuing between a naked and a mailed hand conjoined.* Motto, *Munit haec, et altera vincit.* This jewel was hung from the neck by an orange riband.

Since the union of the three kingdoms, only Baronets of the United Kingdom have been created, and they are distinguished by the silver escutcheon on their arms charged with the Red Hand. In 1929 a badge was authorised to be worn round the neck by Baronets of England, Ireland and the United Kingdom. This consists of the escutcheon of the Red Hand ensigned with the Imperial Crown within a blue oval band ornamented with a gold wavy stem from which issue roses, thistles and shamrocks. The riband is orange edged with blue. This badge may be displayed below the shield of arms.

The badge now worn by Baronets of Nova Scotia consists of the arms as stated above but without crest and supporters and surrounded by a blue oval band inscribed *"Gloria fax mentis honestae".*

Chapter XV

ECCLESIASTICAL HERALDRY

ECCLESIASTICAL heraldry has developed very much along lines of its own, and the results of the absence of effective regulation and control in mediaeval times are apparent to-day. Control by the Sovereign over general armory was exercised, at any rate, by the beginning of the fourteenth century. But the Catholic Church naturally looked to the authority of the Pope for anything that was not of a purely temporal nature. Both the Sovereign and the bishops would tend to regard the armorial matters of the Church as of primarily Church and not State concern. For this reason there was little or no regularised control over ecclesiastical arms in the British Isles until the Reformation and the foundation of a new Protestant Church with the Sovereign as its head. The natural result was that both personal and impersonal arms were assumed for ecclesiastical dignitaries and foundations. This practice was not peculiar to the British Isles, but was also common on the Continent of Europe.

After the Reformation the arms which had been assumed by the Catholic sees were officially recorded and granted to their Protestant successors. These official arms attach to a diocese as a part of the State and the State-established religion. For that reason on the disestablishment of the Scottish and Irish Episcopalian Churches their diocesan arms became extinct and are no longer recognised, though they are still frequently used. On the restoration of the Hierarchy of the Roman Catholic Church to Great Britain it was impossible to obtain arms for the new Catholic sees, since as they did not appertain to the State-established Church they could not be recognised in law. This created considerable difficulty, since the Catholic Church makes more practical use of both personal and impersonal arms than almost any other religious or temporal body. Personal arms can, of course, be obtained, but the necessary delay between application and grant is itself a frequent cause of the assumption of arms.

A new bishop is often a non-armigerous person, but he requires personal arms immediately. They have to be painted on the miniature wine-barrels, the candles and the loaves which he presents to the officiating prelate at his consecration. In addition, one of the first duties of a new bishop is to prepare printed forms for faculties, dispensations, etc., which bear his own name and arms. The heraldic laws of the Catholic

Church are primarily concerned with the insignia displayed with the shield. Except in the case of a papal grant, the Church is not concerned with the actual arms and says that these should comply with the heraldic laws of the country concerned. The arms of the Catholic archiepiscopal see of Westminster were, in fact, granted by a papal brief (Gules, an episcopal staff in pale argent ensigned with a cross pattée or surmounted of a pall of the second fimbriated and fringed of the third and charged with four crosses patée fitchée sable), but, as the grant of a foreign state, they are naturally not recognised by the College of Arms. The position is obviously unsatisfactory, and it would be far better if it could be regularised to avoid the use of what are, in the eyes of the heraldic authorities of the United Kingdom, "bogus" arms. In France and other countries where there is no heraldic authority it is the normal practice for a non-armigerous bishop to invent arms for himself. He has, of course, no other alternative.

The earliest ecclesiastical arms appeared on seals, and these were the personal arms of the bishop or abbot, as the case might be. Seals were made compulsory for all religious authorities and houses in 1237 by the Synod of London, and Edward I in 1307 decreed that each monastery must have a seal, adding that no document would be valid without it. The consequent widespread use of seals was mainly responsible for the assumption of arms by religious establishments. An additional reason for the acquirement of arms was the obligation of producing in respect of the various Church lands, quotas of soldiers who required distinctive banners to fight under.

The use of a common seal resulted in the idea of impersonal arms for religious communities. In many cases the personal arms of bishops and abbots, which had been used on seals during their lifetime, continued in use after their death and gradually acquired the status of impersonal arms. The arms of benefactors to the Church, donors of armorial vestments, etc., and founders of religious houses (sometimes with a difference) were often similarly adopted; whilst some establishments invented arms from the emblems or effigies of the saints in whose honour they were dedicated.

The use of arms for various ecclesiastical purposes spread very rapidly. They were embroidered on the priests' vestments and on the hangings of the altar. They ornamented stained-glass windows and were carved in the stone and woodwork of the churches. They were enamelled on the sacred vessels and were flown as the banner of the community.

Ecclesiastical arms followed the normal heraldic rules and customs as regards composition design and marshalling. An impersonal coat is impaled with a personal one (when they are used together) in the normal

PLATE 20

Gloria Deo

Pro Deo et · Sancto Cuthberto

ECCLESIASTICAL ARMS

Top left: *Arms of Farlham, Bishop of Durham, from the Armorial de Gelre.*
Top right: *Arms of Despenser, Bishop of Norwich, from the Armorial de Gelre.*
Bottom: *Arms of Bishop Wilkinson, Catholic Bishop of Hexham and Newcastle.*

way; that is, the official arms on the dexter side of the shield and the private arms on the sinister. In the Anglican, or Established, Church, the official arms of a diocese are naturally the more important and are frequently used without the personal arms of the bishop. In the Roman Catholic Church, where neither the diocese nor its arms have any recognition in law, the reverse applies; and a bishop will frequently use his personal arms without the assumed arms of his diocese, but with his shield accompanied by the normal emblems of his dignity. In early days either the official or the personal arms were used indifferently, and on seals they were both shown, but on different shields.

The accessories of an ecclesiastical achievement differ considerably from those which normally accompany a shield of arms, and certain of the charges which appear on the shield are peculiar to Church armory. These emblems include the tiara, the ecclesiastical hat, the mitre, the archiepiscopal, etc., crosses, the crozier or pastoral staff, the keys and the pall or pallium.

THE TIARA

The papal tiara is a sort of uncleft mitre of thin metal or of cloth of gold and silver encircled with three open gold crowns of much the same design as the coronet of a marquess. The original headdress of the Bishops of Rome was a high conical cap which was anciently considered in Rome to be a sign of liberty. The first crown to surround it probably made its appearance between the ninth and eleventh centuries, the second was added by Pope Boniface VIII (1294-1303) and the third either by Benedict XI (1303-04) or by Clement V (1305-14). Two bands or tapes are always shown, hanging from the back of the tiara, and it is surmounted by an orb and cross. In the armorial achievement of the Pope, the tiara is placed above his personal arms. It is claimed that the Patriarch of Lisbon was granted the right to use a tiara by Clement XII, but this claim does not seem to be founded in fact. Nevertheless, the Patriarch has displayed a tiara in his achievement for the last two hundred years.

THE ECCLESIASTICAL HAT

The ecclesiastical hat is flat and wide-brimmed with a low crown. On each side hang cords and tassels. The colour of the hat and the number of tassels show the ecclesiastical rank of the wearer. The heraldic use of the hat originated in the red hat of a cardinal, which, as a vestment, is believed to date from its presentation by Innocent IV to the cardinals at the Council of Lyons in 1241. Its red colour is a reminder that its wearers must be ready to shed their blood in defence of the Faith. The cardinal's hat is placed above his shield of arms with fifteen tassels suspended by a fret of cords on each side of the shield. The hats of a patriarch and a primate are green with fifteen green tassels suspended from each side. An archbishop who is not a primate has a green hat with ten green tassels each side. A bishop uses similar colours, but only has six tassels on each side of his hat. Abbots and prelates "nullius" of the Catholic Church have the same hat as a bishop. The green hat is said to be symbolical of the see, which never dies. Ordinary abbots and provosts also wear hats with six tassels each side, but both hat and tassels are black. An abbot of the Premonstratensian Order has a white hat and tassels. A canon has a black hat with three tassels on each side and a simple priest only one.

In the Roman Catholic Church the ecclesiastical hat is rapidly becoming the principle accessory in the achievement owing to the ease with which different grades and classes can be indicated; and the mitre, becoming redundant, is less and less used. In Great Britain ecclesiastical hats are normally displayed above the arms of the Catholic archdioceses and dioceses, except in the case of the diocese of Aberdeen, which uses a mitre only. None of the Church of England sees use the ecclesiastical hat. A detailed list of the ecclesiastical hats used in the Roman Catholic Church is given in the Appendix.

THE MITRE

The mitre does not appear to have come into use before the tenth century, and it was not till the eleventh that it was conferred on bishops outside Rome. It was originally a round bonnet, usually white and bound round the head with an embroidered band, which was at first fastened at the sides but later at the back, with the ends hanging down, and sometimes terminating in small bells. These ends became the labels or *infulae* which still hang from the back of the modern mitre. At the beginning of the twelfth century lobes began to appear above each ear, and gradually rose higher till the mitre was something like the present shape but set sideways on the head. About the middle of the twelfth century a mitre with the vertical points at the front and back began to be worn, and became general about the end of the century. In the fourteenth century the peaks became much taller. In the seventeenth century an ugly type of mitre appeared with swollen bulbous sides. At the present time there is a tendency to return to the lower-peaked Gothic mitre. There are three types of mitre which are known respectively as the *mitra simplex*, the *mitra auirfrigiata* or *auriferata*, and the *mitre pretiosa*. The *mitra simplex* (simple mitre) is made of plain white linen or white silk damask with red fillets. The *mitra auriferata* (gold mitre) is composed of silk damask or cloth of silver and gold but without jewels. The *mitra pretiosa* (precious mitre) is of cloth of gold and ornamented with jewels (properly uncut) and the precious metals. The precious and gold mitres are both worn in turn at different parts of a Pontifical Mass. The gold alone is worn at Confirmation and on certain other occasions. The simple mitre is worn at a Requiem Mass and on Good Friday, and is the mitre ordinarily worn in the presence of the Pope and by prelates below episcopal rank, unless otherwise stipulated.

There is no rule as to which mitre should be represented heraldically when placed above the shield of arms. At the present time Anglican archbishops and bishops always use the gold mitre. The only Catholic dioceses in Great Britain which now show the mitre in their achievement are Lancaster, Argyll and the Isles, and Aberdeen, and all use the precious mitre. The precious mitre, too, is normally used on the Continent of Europe. The Catholic dioceses of Lancaster and Argyll and the Isles are the only ones in Great Britain to include both mitre and ecclesiastical hat in the achievement. The mitre is essentially a pontifical headgear, and where it is worn by abbots and, in certain cases, canons, it is by privilege and not by right.

The mitre of the Bishop of Durham is unique in British heraldry in that it is encircled by a coronet. The reason is that until early in the nineteenth century the see of Durham was also a temporal palatinate, and the coronet denotes the temporal power. In England the mitre of an abbot was frequently placed slightly in profile whilst the mitre of a bishop looked straight to the front, but this rule was never generally observed.

THE ARCHIEPISCOPAL AND OTHER CROSSES

The archiepiscopal cross is a sign of the dignity of an archbishop and it is borne before him in his own province. From about the tenth century this cross was the distinguishing mark of papal legates. Later it was granted to certain primates. About the twelfth century metropolitans were allowed to use it, and finally Pope Gregory IX permitted its use to all archbishops. In addition, in a few specially privileged dioceses the bishops have been granted the right to use the cross. The cross as borne in practice is a crucifix placed on the top of a staff, and it is carried in front of an archbishop and turned towards him. In heraldic use the cross on top of the staff is a plain one, usually patée or bottonny, and it is shown in pale behind the shield. The Catholic diocese of Hexham and Newcastle places the Cross of St. Cuthbert on top of the staff. This is a cross patée with a circle in the centre and with the outer edges of the limbs forming part of the circumference of a circle. At each angle is a ball. This cross is a charge in the arms of the Anglican diocese of Newcastle.

A cross with two bars, or a double traverse, is known as a "primatial" or "patriarchal" cross. It has been used by patriarchs since the fifteenth century and by primates since the seventeenth. (A primate is an archbishop who presides over more than one metropolitan province.) Now, however, all archbishops may place the primatial cross behind their shields. A cross with a treble traverse has frequently been depicted in representations of the papal arms. This is incorrect. The papal cross, if shown at all, should have only a single traverse. The cross with a single traverse, formerly confined to archbishops, is now used heraldically by all bishops. The cross behind the shield denotes episcopal rank and serves to differentiate the arms of a bishop from those of, for instance, a prelate "nullius". Another kind of cross sometimes appears in the arms of archbishops in the British Isles. It is generally shown in pale behind the pallium. This is the archiepiscopal cross as it was originally borne in the fourteenth century before it was placed outside the shield. It is normally described in heraldry as an "Episcopal staff ensigned with a cross patée".

THE CROZIER

The pastoral staff, or crozier, was originally introduced as a walking-staff for aged prelates. It is said to have become a sign of episcopal dignity and jurisdiction in the fourth century and to have been used by abbots in the fifth century. The first croziers appear to have been made of wood or metal with a simple boss at the top of the staff, or a plain curved bend like a walking-stick. The present long staff with its ornamental crook was a later development. It is generally supposed that a bishop's crozier has the end of the crook turned outwards, whilst that of the abbot's is turned inwards towards the staff to show his more limited sphere of authority. Heraldic practice does not, however, seem to support this view. In England the bishop's crozier, when placed behind the shield, was frequently shown with its crook turned outwards, away from the centre of the shield; whilst the abbot's crozier was turned inwards again to show his more limited jurisdiction. This practice, however, was never universally observed. In any case, the crozier of any prelate below the rank of bishop is adequately distinguished by the piece of cloth which should be attached to the staff below the crook. Gloves being episcopal garments, an abbot used this piece of cloth to keep his naked hand from contact with the staff. The normal method of showing the crozier is in pale behind the shield. Most Anglican sees, however, show two croziers in saltire with the mitre placed centrally between them. The see of Durham has a crozier in bend and a sword (the emblem of temporal authority) in bend sinister behind the shield. The Catholic dioceses of Minevia, Nottingham and Plymouth have a crozier in pale placed centrally behind the shield. In the two former the crook is turned to the dexter and in the latter to the sinister. In the Catholic Church, however, the crozier is now generally omitted from episcopal arms when the ecclesiastical hat and cross are used.

THE KEYS

The keys of St. Peter are part of the insignia of the Pope and they are placed in saltire either above or behind his shield and below the tiara, a gold one in bend and a silver one in bend sinister tied together with a red cord. The gold key represents the power which extends to Heaven and the silver the dominion over the faithful on earth. The handles are to the base, for they are in the hends of the Pope. The wards are upwards, for they lock or unlock the gates of Heaven, and they are cut in the shape of a cross to show that their power is obtained from the death of Our Lord. The keys, ensigned with the tiara, are frequently used apart from the arms of the Pope. They are used so as the emblems of the offices of the Roman curia, by apostolic delegations, on the papal flag and, on a red field, as the arms of the Vatican State. Two silver keys in saltire ensigned with an Imperial Crown on a red field are the present arms of the Anglican archdiocese of York. It is probably that these were originally the gold and silver keys of St. Peter and the papal tiara. The old arms of the see of York were identical with those of the see of Canterbury save for one extra cross on the pallium. (Azure, an episcopal staff in pale argent ensigned with a cross patée or, surmounted by a pall of the second, fimbriated and fringed gold, and charged with five crosses patée fitchée.)

From the reign of King Henry I there was bitter rivalry for precedency between the Archbishops of Canterbury and York, which was only settled in Canterbury's favour in 1353. The crossed keys and the tiara appear on the seal of Archbishop Robert Waldby of York (1397 to 1398), so it may well be that the papal insignia were granted as arms to the see of York by the Pope as some compensation. The ancient arms were used on occasions as well as the new ones as late as the time of Archbishop Bowet (1407 to 1423), which lends support to the view that the new arms were an honour.

THE PALLIUM

The pall or pallium is a vestment which only archbishops, and a few bishops by special privilege, are allowed to wear. It is derived from the

PLATE 21

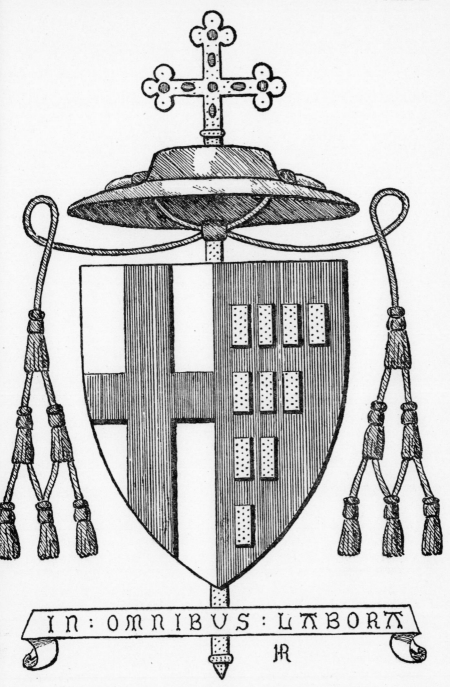

IN : OMNIBVS : LABORA

HR

THE ARMS OF THE ROMAN CATHOLIC BISHOP OF SOUTHWARK

The Arms traditionally used by the diocese (the Cross of St. George) are impaled with the personal arms of the Bishop.

Roman toga and was first given as an honorary distinction. After the seventh century, however, it became a symbol of union with the Holy See, and of the Pope's supreme pastoral power, the acceptance of which implied the acknowledgement of the supremacy of the Pope. The possession of the pallium is necessary to give validity to many of an archbishop's acts; and until he has received his pallium from the Pope he may not use his cross, confer Holy Orders, consecrate a church, etc. The pallium is made of fine white lamb's wool and has on it six crosses patée of black silk edged with cord. As worn, it consists of a flat circular band about three inches in breadth from which hang two strips of the same width as the band, and about a foot long, placed opposite to each other. These strips were originally very long and reached nearly to the ground.

In Continental armory the pallium is represented as of much the same shape as it is actually worn, and it is displayed outside and normally below the shield by residential patriarchs and archbishops. In British heraldry it is the same shape as the ordinary of the same name. It appears in the arms of the archdioceses of Westminster (Roman Catholic), Canterbury (Church of England), Birmingham (Roman Catholic), Cardiff (Roman Catholic), Armagh (Church of Ireland) and Dublin (Church of Ireland). The last two are post-Reformation arms so that in their case the pallium, unlike that of Canterbury, was never a symbol of papal authority. (The arms of Armagh are identical with those of Canterbury, whilst those of Dublin are the same as the ancient arms of York.)

CREST, HELM AND OTHER ACCESSORIES

Ecclesiastics, under British heraldic laws, are entitled to crest and helm, but they are not used with a mitre or ecclesiastical hat. This rule did not always apply, for in the Armorial de Gelre the personal arms of Fordham, Bishop of Durham, and Henry le Despenser, Bishop of Norwich, are shown with helms and mantling, on top of which are mitres with crests rising from the cleft. The base of the Bishop of Durham's mitre is encircled by his coronet. The use of such essentially warlike emblems as helm and crest by an ecclesiastic is now, however, considered to be rather incongruous. Nevertheless, reverend gentlemen have sometimes taken a very active part in war. At the Battle of Bouvines in 1244 the Bishop of Beauvais, one of the six great ecclesiastical peers of France, is said to have despatched several of the enemy with a mace, so as not to break the letter of the law which prohibited the use of the sword by ecclesiastics. In the American Civil War Leonidas Polk, Bishop of Louisiana, was killed in action as a Lieutenant-General in the army of the Confederacy. In the late war that gallant gentleman Admiral d'Argenlieu of the navy of Fighting France was the Carmelite Father Louis of the Trinity, who has since returned to his monastic life.

In modern British grants to a priest the emblazonment includes crest and helm, but in the case of a bishop no helm is shown, and the crest is depicted in the body of the patent.

Arms of the Catholic Church may not be accompanied by any accessories other than the recognised ecclesiastical insignia. Until recently, coronets were allowed to sees which have retained a princely title and to chapters which have a collective title, such as count or baron. Angels are sometimes seen as supporters, but their use is purely decorative and is incorrect. A temporal sword is sometimes authorised amongst the insignia to signify a previous civil jurisdiction, but it should be borne point downwards to show that it refers to a past and not a present jurisdiction. The ecclesiastical accessories must be restricted to those essential to indicate the dignity of the bearer of the arms. The addition of a mitre, for instance, to an achievement which already displays a bishop's hat and cross, is wrong.

If incorrect insignia have been displayed in an achievement for over a hundred years and without protest, the rule of the Catholic Church is that a right to them has been established.

Chapter XVI

ARMS OF CORPORATE BODIES

NOTHING exemplifies more our national love of heraldry than the arms and symbols of the various corporate bodies. Many of them, probably the majority, are either completely bogus or some personal or official arms which have been adopted without authority. A large and growing proportion, however, are legitimate arms, which include many fine examples of heraldic design. It is a pity that so many public bodies, particularly borough, etc., councils, are apparently still unaware that they are displaying arms to which they are not entitled. In this respect Scotland, as in so many other heraldic matters, is far ahead of the remainder of the United Kingdom, due, principally, to the powers vested in the Lord Lyon.

The most familiar of impersonal coats of arms are probably those of the various town and county councils. There is often a great deal of civic pride in the "town arms", as they are frequently called, and they are displayed on the sides of public vehicles, on the official seals, on notices and notepaper, on town halls and, in the case of Liverpool for instance, on roadside sign-boards at the city boundary. These arms generally have some sort of local association.

Associations may be geographical, architectural, historical, religious, ecclesiastical, sporting, in reference to local industries or activities, legendary, family, canting or punning, or descriptive of local amenities. Generally the arms include two or more of the above. Unlike personal arms, it is probable that practically all, if not all, civic arms were based on something of local interest, and that in the case of those which are apparently meaningless the allusion has very likely been forgotten. It is emphasised, incidentally, that arms which are commonly referred to as being those of a particular county, borough, etc., really belong to the local council, as it is not possible to grant arms to a territory.

Examples of the various types of local association seen in civic arms are given below.

GEOGRAPHICAL

London County Council.—*Barry wavy of six azure and argent; on a chief of the second a cross gules charged with a lion of England.*

The wavy blue and silver bars refer to the River Thames.

City of Nottingham.—*Gules, a ragged wooden cross proper, between three open crowns or, the lowest encircling the bottom limb of the cross.* Supporters: *Two royal stage guardant proper, ducally gorged or, each standing on a ragged staff proper.*

The wooden cross, stags and ragged staffs refer to Sherwood Forest.

ARCHITECTURAL

City of Exeter.—*Per pale gules and sable, a triangular castle triple towered or.*

The castle is Rougemont Castle.

City of Norwich.—*Gules, a castle triple towered argent, in base a lion of England.*

The castle is Norwich Castle.

HISTORICAL

Reading.—*Azure, five boys' heads couped proper, the centre one adorned with a Saxon crown or.*

The crowned head is supposed to be that of the Saint King Edward the Martyr, who was murdered by the household of his younger brother whilst on a visit to his mother.

City of Worcester.—*Argent, a fess between three pears sable.*

These commemorate a visit by Queen Elizabeth to the city, when the citizens of Worcester, to mark the occasion, transplanted a pear tree laden with fruit from an orchard to the centre of the town.

RELIGIOUS

Southend-on-Sea.—*Azure, on a pile argent, between in the dexter an anchor, in the sinister a gridiron and in base a trefoil or, three lilies issuing from a vase proper.*

The anchor is the emblem of St. Clement, the patron saint of Leigh, who was supposed to have been bound to an anchor and thrown into the sea. The gridiron is that on which St. Laurence the patron saint of Eastwood was martyred. The trefoil represents the Holy Trinity. The lilies come from the ancient seal of St. Mary's Priory.

Colchester.—*Gules, two ragged staves in cross the arms and the foot pierced by Passion Nails argent, between three crowns or, the lowest encircling the bottom limb of the cross.*

St. Helen, the British mother of the Emperor Constantine, is supposed to have been the daughter of "old King Cole" who is commemorated in the name of the town. St. Helen is the legendary finder of the true cross which the staves and nails represent.

ECCLESIASTICAL

Fulham.—*Barry wavy often argent and azure, on a saltire gules, two swords in saltire the points upwards of the first, enfiled at their intersection with a mitre or.*

Swords in saltire on a red field are the arms of the diocese of London. The mitre refers to the Manor of Fulham, which is held by the Bishops of London.

Gloucester.—*Or, three chevronels gules between ten torteaux, three, three, three, one.*

The ten torteaux are from the diocesan arms of Worcester. The sees of Worcester and Gloucester were at one time united. These arms are of particular interest, as they were granted by the Commonwealth in 1652. Since all Commonwealth grants were declared void at the Restoration, they are not recorded at the College of Arms. Gloucester has an earlier legitimate coat of arms, of a rather complicated design, which was granted in 1538 and is recorded.

SPORTING

Barnes.—*Azure, on a saltire or, between four ostrich feathers argent, two oars in saltire the shafts proper, the blades in chief the dexter dark blue and the sinister light blue.*

The oars refer to the Oxford and Cambridge boat race. The blazon is of interest in that different shades of blue are specified for the oar blades.

Ryde (Isle of Wight).—*Argent, on the sea a schooner rigged yacht in full sail proper, within a bordure azure charged with eight estoiles or.*
The allusion is obvious.

INDUSTRIES AND ACTIVITIES

Swindon.—*Quarterly, the fesswise line nebuly: 1st, Azure, on a pile argent, three crescents gules: 2nd, Gules, three castles one and two argent: 3rd, Gules, a mitre or: 4th, Azure, a winged wheel or: On a chief argent a locomotive engine proper.*

Modern Swindon is, of course, the locomotive headquarters of the Great Western Railway and its successor the Western Region of British Railways. The winged wheel signifies swift railway travel. The locomotive is said to be the old Great Western broad-gauge engine the "Lord of the Isles". It is depicted in various guises: sometimes as a four-coupled compound locomotive of Midland Railway design, which certainly never ran in Great Western colours, and at other times as an engine which equally certainly never ran on any British railway.

Kingston-upon-Thames.—*Azure, three salmon naiant in pale proper.*

A salmon would be a rare catch in the Thames in these days; but the salmon fisheries at Kingston were at one time of great importance.

LEGENDARY

Bradford.—*Per pale gules and azure, on a chevron engrailed between three bugle horns or, a well sable.* Crest: *a boar's head without tongue erased Scottish fashion argent, in front of a tree trunk with leaves sprouting therefrom proper.*

As part of the service which one John Northrop of Manningham paid to John Gaunt for his lands, was "One blast with his horn upon St. Martin's Day". The blowing of a horn in the Market Place every St. Martin's Day became a custom. These lands are said to have been the reward offered for the death of a boar, which had become something of a local terror. The boar was slain by a youth whilst drinking at a well, which was later called "Boar's Well". The youth cut out the boar's tongue and brought it back to support his claim for the reward. A man, who came across the dead boar later, cut off its head and also claimed the reward. The tongue, however, was indisputable proof of the youth's claim and the man was punished.

Bury St. Edmunds.—*Azure, three crowns each pierced by two arrows in saltire the points downwards or.* Crest: *A wolf sejant holding between its forepaws the crowned head of St. Edmund proper.*

The blue field and gold crowns were the arms assigned by the mediaeval heralds to the Kings of the East Angles, and they are particularly associated with St. Edmund, who was the last East Anglican King. King Edmund was defeated and killed by the Danes in 868, dying as a martyr for his Faith. He is stated to have been shot with arrows and then beheaded. His followers recovered his body but were unable to find his head until, guided by the voice of the dead King, they came upon it guarded by a wolf.

FAMILY

Buckingham.—*Per pale sable and gules, a swan with wings displayed and inverted argent, ducally gorged or.*

The tinctures of the field are the livery colours of the Staffords, Dukes of Buckingham. The swan is the famous de Bohun badge which, as has already been mentioned, the Staffords inherited.

147

Warrington.—*Ermine, six lioncels gules, within a bordure azure, charged with eight covered cups or.*

The lioncels are taken from the arms of Pain de Vilars, baron in the time of Henry I; Warrington being the centre of the baronial estates. The covered cups are from the canting arms of the Botelers who succeeded to the barony.

CANTING OR PUNNING

City of Liverpool.—*Argent, a liver (cormorant) with a piece of laver (seaweed) in its beak proper.*

Both the liver and laver allude to the name of the city.

City of Oxford.—*Argent, the base barry wavy of eight azure and of the field, supporting an ox passant gules.*

The heraldic representation of water is, of course, allusive to the "ford" in the name of the city. These arms are one of the most familiar of the civic coats from their appearance on successive incarnations of a famous brand of motor-car.

City of Bath.—*Azure, in chief two barrulets wavy, in base a stone wall embattled argent, over all a sword in pale the blade gules, the hilt in base or.*

The silver wavy barrulets in blue, and the embattled wall together refer to the famous Roman baths of Aquae Sulis.

Bournemouth.—*Quarterly, or and azure, a cross patonce between 1st and 4th, a lion rampant holding a rose; 2nd, six martlets; 3rd, four fish naiant in pale, all counterchanged. Crest: At the base of a pine tree proper, four roses fesswise or.*

The blue and gold colour-scheme is supposed to refer to Bournemouth's sand, blue sky and sea. The sea is further emphasised by the fish. The martlets, interpreted as sand martins, suggest the sand cliffs. But the cross patonce, martlets and tinctures were taken in the first instance from the arms of St. Edward the Confessor, since Bournemouth and the surrounding district constituted one of his Royal demesnes. The lion recalls the warlike character of the coastline in mediaeval times. The pine tree and roses stand for the beauty and health-giving properties of Bournemouth. Altogether this is a very effective heraldic advertisement.

The civic arms of England and Wales and their origin are very fully described by Mr. C. Wilfrid Scott-Giles in his beautifully illustrated book, *Civic Heraldry.*

Until the grouping of the railways in 1923 the arms borne by the

PLATE 22

THE ARMORIAL ACHIEVEMENT OF THE GREAT NORTHERN RAILWAY (IRELAND)

There are certain heraldic objections to the arms used by this railway, but they are of interest as being typical of the designs adopted by the old private companies, and they make a very handsome addition to the attractive livery of the Great Northern's locomotives and carriages.

old companies were probably as well known to the general public as those of their home town. The railway arms frequently decorated the outside of the carriages and the tenders or wheel splashers of the loco-motives, and were liberally displayed on refreshment-room crockery, timetables and station buildings. Most of these arms were assumed, and generally consisted of the arms of the principal towns served by the railway, marshalled in different ways.

The method of marshalling, however, was not always heraldically correct, and civic arms were sometimes incorrectly rendered.

The Great Northern Railway provided an example of a most ambi-tious but unfortunate design. The arms of the City of London, complete with bogus crest and supporters, were at the top. Below these were a thistle and rose, slipped and leaved, in saltire. Below the thistle and rose were three quartered shields placed one and two. The first shield bore the Royal Arms of England and Scotland (the latter without the tressure), the hunting scene from the seal of Huntingdon, and the earlier and unauthorised arms of Peterborough. The dexter shield bore the arms of Grantham, Nottingham, Sheffield (complete achievements of the two latter were emblazoned, each on one quarter of the shield) and Man-chester. The sinister shield displayed the arms of Doncaster, the com-plete achievement of Leeds, the arms of York and the arms of Bradford. Between the two lower shields was an escutcheon of the unauthorised arms of Wakefield. Such a combination of armorial error, bogus arms and incorrect draughtsmanship can seldom have been equalled. In a later design the Company was content to display the Royal Arms of England and Scotland (the latter still bereft of the tressure) side by side on an extremely ugly background.

A very pleasant example of an achievement showing the arms of towns was that of the Highland Railway, which embodied the arms of Perth and Inverness. The arms of the City of Perth are surmounted on the breast of a double-headed eagle. In the achievement of the railway company the two shields are placed accolée on a single-headed eagle displayed with wings inverted, and the whole is surrounded by a belt and buckle inscribed "Highland Railway Company". The arms of Perth and Inverness are both unusual in design and embody religious subjects. The official blazon of the former is, "Gules, a holy lambe passant regardant staff and cross argent, with the banner of St. Andrew proper, all within a double tressure counter-flowered of the second". The arms of the Royal Burgh of Inverness are, "Gules, our Lord upon the Cross proper".

The arms used by the Great Northern Railway of Ireland, the last of the great private companies, are, "Quarterly, 1st Dublin, 2nd Londonderry, 3rd Enniskillen, 4th Belfast; overall on an inescutcheon gold the hand gules of Ulster; the whole surrounded by a garter inscribed Great Northern Railway (Ireland)".

A cleverly designed coat of arms was granted to the Great Central Railway on 25th February 1898. The official blazon is, "Argent, a cross gules, voided of the field between two wings in chief sable and as many daggers erect in base of the second, in the fess point a morion winged of the third; on a chief also of the second a pale of the first, thereon eight arrows saltirewise banded also of the third, between on the dexter side three bendlets enhanced and on the sinister a fleur-de-lis or. Crest: on a wreath of the colours, a representation of the front of a locomotive engine proper, between two wings or." The crest is, in fact always depicted as a "locomotive engine affronté", and so it should be blazoned, because the "front of a locomotive engine" is a far too elastic term, and might restrict the view to the buffer beam. In any case the front of a thing could hardly be modelled in the round. The red voided cross, the daggers and the wings all refer to the arms of the City of London, which are, "Argent, a cross and in the first quarter a sword erect point upwards gules. Crest: a dragon's wing argent, charged with a cross gules; Supporters: two dragons, wings elevated and addorsed argent, and charged with a cross gules". The crest and supporters are, strangely enough, bogus, although the arms themselves are genuine.

The development of the fan crest into a dragon's wing has already been mentioned, and it is probable that the dragon supporters owe their origin to the assumed crest. The sword in the arms is the emblem of St. Paul, patron of the City of London; a sword having been the instrument of the saint's martyrdom. The wings in the arms of the Great Central Railway are dragon's wings and are taken from the crest of the City of London, and the blazon should, of course, specify the type of wing. It is peculiar, however, that the College of Arms should have used an unauthorised crest as the basis of a charge to represent London. On some representations of the Great Central arms the wings are drawn more like sea shells. The winged morion is the hat of Mercury, and represents speed. The arrows represent Sheffield, whose arms are, "Per fess azure and vert, in chief eight arrows saltirewise banded argent, in base three garbs or". The bendlets come from the arms of Manchester, "Gules, three bendlets enhanced or; on a chief argent a ship in full sail on the sea." The fleur-de-lis represents the arms of Wakefield, which are, "Azure, a fleur-de-lis or, fimbriated ermine". The Great Central's motto is "Forward".

There are signs of the influence of these arms in the beautiful achievement which was granted to the company's succcessors, the London and

North Eastern Railway. The same motto is used, and the figure of Mercury supported by a cloud appears as the crest. The arms are based on those of the city of York, which are "Argent, on a cross gules, five lions of England." In the L.N.E.R. arms the centre lion is replaced by a triple-towered castle. In the first and fourth quarters is a griffin segreant sable, in the second a rose and in the fourth a thistle, both the latter being slipped and leaved. The shield is supported by two lions, the dexter one guardant. It is unfortunate that this attractive coat should not have been used more frequently than it was.

The Caledonian Railway embellished its locomotives and carriages with the complete Scottish Royal achievement, including the jewel and motto of the Order of the Thistle. Below, but forming part of the design, was a scroll inscribed "Caledonian Railway Company". There was presumably some authority for the use of the Royal Arms, for it could hardly have escaped the notice of the Lord Lyon.

The aristocratic London and North Western used a circular red field charged with the seated figure of Britannia, with her shield of the Union devine in front of a couchant lion, of gold. Around this was such a mass of ornamental scroll-work that the whole design looked rather like a green vegetable. One class of six-coupled goods engines which bore this device were (and still are) known, in fact, as the "Cauliflowers".

The only one of the four great post-grouping companies to display arms to any great extent was the Great Western, which placed the arms and crests of the cities of London and Bristol side by side on carriages and passenger locomotives. The Great Western had used these arms for many years before the grouping. The London Midland and Scottish had an odd device which could hardly be considered armorial. The nationalised British Railways have not obtained a grant of arms, although they use the lion and wheel emblem of the British Transport Commission. The only nationalised transport concern to receive a grant of arms so far is British European Airways.

Most of the great schools and colleges bear arms, some, unfortunately, without authority. Wellington College uses the arms of the Duke of Wellington. Ampleforth College received a very effective coat in 1912. These are, "Per fess indented, or and azure; a chief parted per pale, dexter gules, the keys of St. Peter; sinister the arms of St. Edward the Confessor". The arms of Eton College, which were granted in 1449, are "Sable, three lilies argent: a chief parted per pale, dexter, azure, a fleur-de-lis or; sinister, gules, a lion of England". The lilies are symbolical of Our Lady, for the full title of Eton is the "College of the Blessed Mary of Eton". The chief, which incorporates part of the then Royal Arms, refers to the founder, King Henry VI.

Some of the recent corporation and company arms are fine examples of heraldic design. The arms of the Auctioneers' and Estate Agents' Institute of the United Kingdom, granted in 1927, are "Per chevron or and azure, in chief two trees proper, in base a castle triple towered argent. Crest: A gavel erect or, between two wings displayed and addorsed gules".

Chapter XVII

ARMORIAL SEALS

THE use of seals was established very early in the history of civilisation, and in Babylon, Egypt, Assyria, China and other ancient countries persons of standing had their private seals with which they gave their authority or agreement to documents and which they used to mark their private property. The art of the seal engraver was early established, for there was naturally a demand for devices which could not easily be forged, and the earliest engraved stones are of Babylonian and Egyptian origin. Since it was such an easy way of signifying a King's authority to the remotest parts of his dominion, the engraved seal soon came to be one of the symbols of supreme power and majesty, and has so remained till the present day. Armory, when it arrived, found a ready employment in seals, for every person of any standing or property had his own seal, which he used as his signature. Very soon arms served as essential a purpose on seals as they did in battle and tournament. Much of our knowledge of mediaeval heraldry has been obtained from a study of armorial seals. They show the development of crests, supporters and mantling; the type of helm, armour, shield and caparisons of a charger; the early methods of marshalling arms; the history of individual arms; the development of armorial design and many other matters of importance to heraldry and its associated subjects.

THE GREAT SEALS, OR SEALS OF MAJESTY, OF ENGLAND

"The KING has been pleased by Letters Patent under the Great Seal bearing date .... to appoint, etc." This is a formula which may be seen often in the *London Gazette*. The Great Seal is a large affair which may measure anything between four and six inches in diameter. The matrix (the seal itself, as opposed to its impression) consists of two parts, the obverse and the reverse, each engraved with a different design. These designs are impressed on each side of the wax, which is suspended below the document it seals.

The present series of the Great Seals of the English monarchy really starts with that of King Edward the Confessor of 1043. The obverse of this shows the King seated on the throne holding the sceptre and orb. On the reverse he is also seated on the throne, but he holds a sceptre surmounted by a dove of peace and mercy in one hand and the sword of justice in the other. The seals of the Norman Kings from William the

Conqueror to Henry II are of poor design, but they introduced a form which was retained for very many reigns. The King is enthroned on the obverse and mounted on a horse, clad in armour on the reverse. The seal of William II is of interest as it is the first to display a badge. This is the "sixfoil rose-en-soleil" mentioned in Chapter XI. This seal is also the first to be inscribed with the formula "Dei Gratia", which, with rare exceptions, has continued in use until the present day. The Great Seal of King Richard Cœur de Lion is the first to include a coat of arms. The equestrian figure of the King on the reverse carries a shield emblazoned with a lion rampant to the sinister. Only half of the curved shield is visible and, as stated in Chapter XIII, it is conjectured that a lion rampant was charged on the sinister half. This seal was lost at sea and Richard Cœur de Lion's second one of 1197 is charged with the arms which he had presumably adopted sometime previously and which are still the Royal Arms of England.

On the seals of Edward I and Edward II there are two small lions, one on each side of the throne and stretching up towards it. On the reverse the bardings of the charger are emblazoned with the arms of England, and the King has a coronet round the helm and carries the attractive heater-shaped shield. Edward II's seal was the same as his father's except that he used his mother's badge of Castile, a small castle, as a difference.

King Edward III had no less than eight Great Seals during his reign, and this was also the best period of the seal engraver's art. The first was the same as that of Edward I and II except that he added a fleur-de-lis to the castle, in reference to his mother's country of France. The second was notable for its magnificent Gothic throne. The third was a seal of absence, that is, one prepared for temporary use during the King's absence from the country. It was the same design as the second except for the omission of a canopy over the throne. On the fourth seal the arms of France ancient were quartered with those of England for the first time and the title "Rex Franciae" was added to the inscription. The fifth was another seal of absence and showed a further development of the Gothic architecture of the throne. The sixth, which is illustrated, was very like the fifth. There are lions seated on each side of the throne and on the reverse the helm is surmounted by a chapeau on which is the crest. The seventh is the so-called "Brétigny Seal", which is noted for the excellence of its design. It was produced to celebrate the Peace of Brétigny, and the title to the French throne was omitted. The eighth was the same, but the French title is restored. This design was used by King Richard II and on the first seal of King Henry IV.

King Henry IV's second seal was the so-called "Golden Seal", which was made, as its name implies, of gold, and rivalled the Brétigny Seal in beauty of design. The new arms of France ("France modern") made their first appearance on this seal. The Golden Seal design was retained by King Henry V and also by King Henry VI, but the latter used the reverse of the Brétigny matrix with the addition of a quatrefoil. Henry VI used a plainer seal for French affairs. On the obverse the arms of France were placed on the dexter side of the throne and France quartered with England on the sinister side.

On the seal of Edward IV were several suns in radiance in commemoration of the "mock suns" he claimed to have seen in the sky before his victory at the Battle of Mortimer's Cross. Edward IV's seals, however, were of poor design and they have been called inferior imitations of the Gothic masterpieces. Nevertheless, they were used with little alteration until and including the first seal of Henry VIII. This had a peculiarity in that whilst a fleur-de-lis was used as a badge of France, England was represented by a lion *rampant*. The second seal of Henry VIII, the last of the Gothic Great Seals, included the new Royal title of "Fidei Defensor" which had recently been awarded to him by the Pope. The saddle cloth of the horse on the reverse of Queen Mary's first seal was powdered with the castles and pomegranates of Castile and Aragon in allusion to her mother. Behind the horse was a large fleur-de-lis. On her second seal the arms of Spain were displayed on the obverse impaling those of France and England. On the reverse the bardings of the horse were diapered with castles, roses, fleurs-de-lis and roundels. The background was similarly strewn, with the addition of pomegranates. Queen Elizabeth's second seal was noteworthy for the first appearance as a Royal badge of the crowned harp of Ireland, which was engraved on the reverse together with the rose and fleur-de-lis. Her special seal for Ireland, incidentally, bore an uncrowned harp.

THE GREAT SEALS OF SCOTLAND

The Great Seals of Scotland generally follow a similar trend to those of England, but the standard of excellence generally remains in a more consistently high level. The series properly starts with the seal of King Duncan II, which is of somewhat primitive design and shows the King on a charger in armour of Norman pattern. King Eadgar is seated on a throne on his seal wearing a crown and holding a sceptre. The seal of Alexander I heralded a fashion which was the reverse of the English; the equestrian figure was on the obverse and the throne on the reverse. The mounted figure of Alexander holds a shield and a gonfanon with three streamers. On the reverse he is seated on his throne holding sword

PLATE 23

THE REVERSE OF THE GOLDEN SEAL 1408-48 USED BY KINGS HENRY IV, HENRY V
AND HENRY VI

and orb, and there is a badge of a roundel charged with a rosette. King David I had a similar design. William the Lion's followed the same plan but was a much finer production. Arms first appeared on the Great Seal of Alexander II. The shield of the equestrian figure and the bardings of the horse are charged with a rampant lion. No tressure is visible, but there are faint marks on the shield which may be the remains of one. The first seal of Alexander III is similar, but on the bardings of the horse the lion is within a bordure of which the inner edge is ornamented with fleurs-de-lis, and there are apparent signs of the double tressure on the shield. Panels are included which are each charged with a leopard's face. The second is a great improvement on the first. The double tressure appears in the arms, and the helm of the equestrian figure is surmounted by a panache plume. The background of both the obverse and reverse is powdered with trefoils. These have already been mentioned in connection with Scottish Royal badges in Chapter XI.

The next Great Seal was that of the First Interregnum, 1291-92. It is a beautiful piece of work with a shield of the Scottish Royal Arms in the obverse and St. Andrew on his cross on the reverse. The background on both sides is again semé of trefoils. The equestrian figure in John Balliol's seal has a crowned helm. On the reverse there is a shield with the Balliol orle on the dexter side of the throne and another with the rampant lion but no apparent tressure on the sinister side. The seal of the Second Interregnum shows King Edward I enthroned on one side and a shield of the arms of England on the other. The Scottish badge of the thistle, as already stated, makes its first appearance on the second seal of Robert Bruce. King David II, who was a minor, is shown on his throne on the obverse, and there is a shield of arms on the reverse. The seal of King Robert II is very like the sixth of King Edward I of England. Eagles support the shields in the side niches of the throne, and the mounted figure of the King is in plate armour, wearing a crest on the helm. Robert III's is similar, but there is a pierced mullet over the crested helm. The seal of James I was also very similar. James II adopted it, but added two small annulets between the King's feet and the lions beneath them. James III used the same design with a mullet over the pinnacle of the throne and a fleur-de-lis under the horse's right foot. James IV added still more marks for difference, and James V retained the same design with yet further additions. The second seal of James V was a rather poor copy of the first, but is noteworthy for the re-appearance of the slipped trefoil.

Queen Mary used many seals. On the reverse the Royal Arms were supported by two unicorns. Her seal as Dowager of France has the trefoil badge on it, and the arms of Scotland and France dimidiated on

PLATE 24

ENGLISH AND SCOTTISH GREAT SEALS

Top: *Seal of "Government of the Realm", showing obverse and reverse, Scottish Interregnum 1291-92. Note trefoils on background of seal.*

Bottom: *Sixth seal of King Edward III, showing obverse and reverse, 1340-60. Note (i) Arms of France Ancient quartered with England, (ii) Lions on either side of throne, (iii) Crest and Chapeau worn on helm.*

a shield which is supported by unicorns holding banners charged with St. Andrew'a saltire. James VI had a somewhat similar design on the reverse of his Scottish seal except that the arms of France were not included on the shield, and he used as badges the thistle and a plume of ostrich feathers.

BRITISH GREAT SEALS

There is not much of armorial interest in the Great Seals after the union of the two crowns, and it is not proposed to consider them at any great length. James VI of Scotland ascended the throne of England as James I and his seal shows the arms of the two countries, and in addition a banner of the fanciful arms of Cadwallader, last King of the Britons and common ancestor of the two Royal houses. On the equestrian side there is a greyhound by the King's horse. Cromwell's Great Seal has the arms of the Commonwealth on the reverse with his own on an inescutcheon of pretence. The crest is a lion passant guardant crowned, and the supporters a crowned lion and dragon.

The first proclamation of King Charles II made use of this Commonwealth seal. On the fourth seal of Charles II there are two eagles each holding the Union flag. The seal of William and Mary omitted the arms of Scotland because, at the time it was made, they had not been declared rulers of that country. On Anne's second seal the figure of Britannia is seated on a rock with her oval shield, which displays the impaled arms of the two kingdoms. The fourth Great Seal of George III omits France from the arms for the first time since the Peace of Brétigny, and includes the arms of Ireland.

Lord Campbell in his introduction to the *Lives of the Lord Chancellors* says of the Great Seal, "It is considered the emblem of sovereignty, the *clavis regni*, the only instrument by which on solemn occasions the will of the sovereign can be expressed. Absolute faith is universally given to every document purporting to be under the Great Seal, as having been duly sealed with it by the authority of the Sovereign."

OTHER OFFICIAL SEALS

The other official seals of the Kingdom which are used, or have been used in the past, include the Royal Signets, the Privy Seal, the Royal Courts of Exchequer, Royal Courts of the King's Bench, the Court of Common Pleas, the Steward and Marshal of the Royal Household, and several others. In all of these armorial devices play a prominent part.

The Royal Signet seals have varied in diameter from a half to one and a half inches. The principal design is generally the shield of arms with a crown between the initials of the Sovereign. Henry V placed palm branches on each side of the shield and used the lions of England only. Richard III surrounded it with a collar of roses with the "George" pendant therefrom. Henry VIII used the collar of SS. Charles I was the first to surround his shield with the Garter. Cromwell used his family arms of six quarterings, of which five were Welsh. Signets are used as follows: A Warrant is signed by the Sovereign, counter-signed by the Secretary of State or Lords of the Treasury and is called a "Sign Manual". It is then directed to the Attorney or Solicitor-General requiring the preparation of a bill for Royal signature. When prepared it is signed by the Law Officer and Sovereign and is called a "signet bill". It is then taken to the Signet Office, where an attested copy is made and addressed to the Lord Privy Seal. To this copy the Sovereign's Signet, which is in the possession of the Secretary of State, is affixed. A similar copy signed with the Privy Seal is sent to the Lord Chancellor.

The Privy Seal is usually used to authorise the employment of the Great Seal. The standard design is a shield of the Royal Arms with a legend in the margin. The first seal of James I includes the rose-en-soleil badge surrounded by the King's name and titles. On his second seal the shield is supported by lions and the design incorporates the ostrich-feather badge.

The seal of the Royal Court of the Queen's Bench normally shows the Sovereign enthroned on the obverse and the Royal Arms on the reverse. Henry VI's seal includes the badge of a leopard's face. The shield on Henry VIII's seal is supported by a crowned lion and a wyvern. The seal of the Court of Common Pleas is much the same, but has been more prolific in badges. Rose, fleur-de-lis, rose-en-soleil, star, lion of England, pomegranate and annulet have all been used. That used during the reign of Philip and Mary shows the two monarchs on thrones on the obverse, and on the reverse the Royal Arms of Spain impaling those of England. The shield is supported by a crowned eagle and a collared greyhound. On Queen Mary's earlier seal there is a rose tree and a pomegranate tree in fruit.

The seal of the Royal Court of the Exchequer from Edward I to Henry VIII has an equestrian design on the obverse and a shield of arms on the reverse. On the second seal of Henry VIII the upper half of the field on the obverse is in chequy, the small squares alternately plain and charged with fleurs-de-lis. This was in reference to the Exchequer.

Early official seals of the fourteenth and fifteenth centuries, such as those of the Stewards and Marshals of the Royal Household, frequently bore composed arms—a combination of the personal arms of the office holder and the arms of England.

OTHER SEALS

The early seals of the landed proprietors and noblemen were generally equestrian. From the time of the Norman Conquest until the beginning of the twelfth century they were very crude. In the thirteenth century there was a great improvement in design, and the use of armorial achievements became frequent. A counter seal, or reverse, was often used and was generally embellished with a shield of the arms. A very fine example is the seal of Humphrey de Bohun, Earl of Hereford, in 1259. The obverse is equestrian with arms on the shield and bardings of the horse. On the reverse is a shield of arms with the de Bohun swan above it. On either side is a small shield charged with a cross and ensigned with a trefoil. The fourteenth century was the best period of design, and, as we have already seen, crest, helm and supporters began to accompany the shield of arms. At the same time the equestrian type started to decline, and by the end of the century it was little used, though some families retained it for many years. Until the end of the fifteenth century shield design on seals followed, naturally, the types in practical use.

About the middle of the fourteenth century the beautiful combination of a heater-shaped shield placed couché beneath crest and helm became popular. The heraldic art displayed in some of these achievements has seldom been equalled. Towards the end of the fifteenth century the à bouche shield became common. The Renaissance brought a sad decline in the standard of design. The display of quarterings became customary and a shield which, except for curved corners and points at its base, was almost square was introduced to accommodate them. A dull flatness replaced the grace, boldness and beauty of the Gothic designs. The shapeless shields were soon accompanied with impossible crests and the deep engraving of the early craftsman was superseded by shallow medal-like impressions.

Whilst the baronial seals were round, those of religious offices and houses were generally vesica shaped; that is to say, the perimeter was formed by two arcs of a circle meeting at a point at the top and bottom. This form was supposed to have been derived from the fish symbol of the Catacombs. The most typical characteristic of ecclesiastical seals from the earliest period till the sixteenth century is the figure of the bishop, abbot, etc., with the hand raised in blessing. No shields of arms were engraved on the first seals, but the later ones were rich in armory. As stated in Chapter XV, seals were made compulsory for all religious houses in 1237. Some of them are extremely interesting. The Vice-Warden of the Cambridge Grey Friars, for instance, used, about 1244, a vesica-shaped seal bearing the arms bestowed by the heralds on Our Lord: "A cross raguly debruised by a spear and a crown of thorns in bend dexter and a sponge on a staff in bend sinister, between two three-fold flagella in base." Arms on episcopal seals were usually accompanied by a mitre which was placed above the shield. The seals used by the Bishops of Durham as Counts Palatine were of the normal baronial equestrian type. The helm was encircled by a coronet and surmounted by a crest or plumed mitre. The bishop's personal arms were borne on the shield and on the bardings of the horse. After the Reformation the composition and the proportions of ecclesiastical seals deteriorated. The puritanical zeal of the reformers led to some hasty changes. In 1544 a scene of the Annunciation on the seal of the see of Norwich was replaced by a shield of arms!

Ladies also generally used the vesica shape. A popular type showed the figure of the owner erect, holding a shield of her husband's arms on one side and her own on the other. Sometimes ladies are depicted in a heraldic gown or mantle emblazoned with the married achievement, and the arms appear again on a shield on the reverse. Equestrian seals for ladies are comparatively rare.

A notable lady's seal is that of Ela Basset, daughter of William Longespée, Countess of Warwick, widow of the Earl Thomas de New-burgh and wife of Philip Basset. She died about 1297. She is depicted on a vesica-shaped seal holding a shield of the Longespée arms (Azure, six lioncels or) in her left hand. In the field is a shield of the arms of the earldom of Warwick. On the reverse are the arms of Basset (Or, three bars wavy gules) between two of the Longespée lioncels.

Many people in a position to require the use of seals, such as the smaller landowners, were non-armigerous, and they display a wide variety of devices, many of which are armorial in character.

One of the largest classes of seals consists of those used for towns, corporations, schools, universities, etc. Many of them bore arms from an early date. Others bore devices or pictorial representations of some event which have formed the basis of later grants of arms. The fourteenth-century seal of the city of Oxford, for instance, shows an ox passing a ford. In the background is an oak tree and on the dexter side a shield charged with a cross. The ox and ford, as we saw in the last chapter, have now been incorporated in the city arms. The thirteenth-century seal of Colchester bears on the reverse the effigy of St. Helen enthroned and holding a long cross. The present arms of Colchester representing the True Cross have also been described. Religious subjects are the most common on the early seals of the universities. Jesus College, Cambridge, has on its seal of 1496 a shield of another coat of arms bestowed by the

Plate 25

MISCELLANEOUS SEALS

GREAT SEAL OF THE SECOND SCOTTISH INTERREGNUM, 1296-1306
Obverse: *King Edward I of England*
Reverse: *Arms of England*

SEAL OF JEANNE DE CHATILLON, WIFE OF PIERRE, COUNT OF ALENÇON, DAUGHTER
AND HEIRESS OF JEAN, COUNT OF BLOIS, 1271

SEAL OF HUMPHREY DE BOHUN, EARL OF HEREFORD, 1259
Note the swan of the de Bohuns above the shield

heralds on Our Lord. These are, "A human heart between two couped hands and as many feet in saltire, gouttées de sang".

Sigillography, or the study of seals, is, even when confined to the armorial aspect, a very big subject, and it is only possible to give a very brief outline in one chapter. It may possibly claim to be the oldest hobby in the world, for the collection of seals became a craze in ancient Rome and Julius Caesar himself seems to have been a collector.

Chapter XVIII

ARMORIAL COINS

EVICES were struck on coins very early in their history. The city states of ancient Greece used their own emblems on their coinage. Athens used an owl; Corinth, a pegasus; Aegina, a turtle; Chalcis, a wheel; Eretria, a gorgon head; Cyzicus, a tunny fish; Phocaea, a seal. Badges were not used on the coins of Republican and Imperial Rome, but there are many of the symbols which were subsequently adopted by heraldry: the cornucopia, or horn of plenty; the caduceus, or staff of Mercury, messenger of the gods; the Imperial eagle; the fasces: the pegasus; the thunderbolt, symbol of divinity; the scales, emblems of justice; the seated figure of Britannia; and several others.

Our own coinage starts with the Anglo-Saxon issues. They were crude, and few are of any heraldic, or rather pre-heraldic, interest. The silver penny of Offa, King of Mercia, is noteworthy in that its influence in design has persisted up to our own times. On the reverse is a small cross with five roundels in each of the angles. On Aethelred II's London penny there is a larger voided cross, but with nothing in the angles. St. Edward the Confessor's penny has another voided cross with a martlet in each of the angles. (Hence the arms allotted to him by the heralds.) The cross appears on coins of the Norman Kings, and on pennies of King Stephen it is accompanied by fleurs-de-lis. The reverse of King Henry II's first penny is charged with a cross potent between four saltires potent—very similar to the arms of Jerusalem. There is a voided cross with roundels in the angles on the later pennies of Henry II and on these of John and Henry III. On King Henry III's golden penny there is a rose between each set of three roundels. Edward I introduced a cross with three roundels in each angle, and this remained the standard design on the reverse of pennies and groats up to the first issues of King Henry VII.

King Edward III's gold noble is a fine design. On the obverse the King is seen in a ship holding a sword erect and a shield of the quartered arms of France and England. On the reverse is an ornamental cross with a fleur-de-lis at the end of each arm, the initial of the King in the centre, and a trefoil, a lion of England and an open crown in each angle. This coin is supposed to commemorate the naval victory of Sluys in 1340. The same design was used for the noble until the reign of Henry VI, save for changes in the name and initial of the King and the alteration of the arms of France from ancient to modern. Edward IV's rose noble is very similar, but there is a slight decline in the artistic standard. On the obverse a banner with the letter E is in the stern of the ship and the hull is charged with a rose. The cross on the reverse has the same terminations to the arms, but the centre is occupied by the rose-en-soleil. The trefoils below the lions are omitted. Edward IV's gold angel has St. Michael killing the dragon on the obverse, and on the reverse a ship charged with a shield of the Royal Arms above which is a cross between the letter E and a rose.

Henry VII produced a very fine gold sovereign. On the obverse the King is seated on an ornamental throne in the Renaissance style. On each side is a pillar, the dexter surmounted with a seated greyhound and the sinister with a dragon. The background is semé-de-lis. On the reverse is a Tudor rose charged in the centre with a shield of the Royal Arms.

Henry VII's groats, half-groats and pennies of 1504 and later start a new fashion in English coinage. For the first time there is a profile portrait which is a likeness of the King, instead of the conventional affronté crowned head which had so far been used. On the reverse the cross remains, but it is surmounted with a shield of the Royal Arms so that the cross continues the lines of the quartering, and each quarter covers the angle of the cross previously occupied by the roundels. Cardinal Wolsey's "York" half-groat of Henry VIII's reign is of interest. The design is the same as that of Henry VII's 1504 series, but on one side of the shield on the reverse is the letter T and on the other the letter W, the initial letters of Thomas Wolsey. Below the shield is a cardinal's hat.

Philip and Mary's shilling shows a shield of the impaled arms of France and England on the reverse. Elizabeth's coins have a rose behind the profile head on the obverse, and the shield and cross on the reverse. The mill, or machine-made, coin was first introduced in Elizabeth's reign, and this method entirely supplanted the old hammered coinage in the reign of King Charles II.

Scottish coins are very similar to the English, with the same cross design on the reverse. In the early issues from David I to David II, however, a profile portrait is used and mullets are placed in the angles of the cross. Robert II's coins copied the English style entirely. James IV's 18-shilling piece was known as a "unicorn", from a representation of the mythical animal on the obverse supporting a shield of the Scottish arms.

King John's Dublin penny shows the King's head inside a triangle in the obverse with a quatrefoil in the sinister base angle. Another triangle on the reverse encloses the sun-star and crescent badge of the Plantagenets. King Edward IV's Irish half-groat has the English shield and cross on the obverse, and a cross surmounted by the three St. Edmund's crowns on the reverse. Edward IV's Dublin groat was the same as the standard English pattern, whilst his Drogheda groat only differed from it in the substitution of a rose in the centre of the cross on the obverse for the roundels in the angles.

With the accession to the English throne of King James of Scotland, the Scottish arms, and also the Irish, appear for the first time on the English coinage. The shield of arms on the reverse of James I's shillings displays France quartered with England in the first and fourth grand quarters, Scotland in the second grand quarter and Ireland in the third. The cross is absent, but it reappears in conjunction with the same shield on the shilling of Charles I.

The first Commonwealth design has the shield of St. George within a wreath on the obverse, and the same shield placed accolée with another charged with the harp of Ireland on the reverse. Later Commonwealth coins have the profile head of Oliver Cromwell on the obverse, and on the reverse a shield of the peculiar Commonwealth arms mentioned in Chapter XIII, ensigned with an Imperial Crown!

Charles II introduced the four shields arranged in the shape of a cross, instead of the combination of shield and cross which was still a feature of our florins in very recent years.

The familiar seated figure of Britannia with her shield, modelled from the King's favourite, the Duchess of Richmond, was first seen on Charles II's farthing. William III inserted the arms of Nassau in the middle of the four crosswise shields. An unusual guinea was minted in the reign of George III. On the reverse is a heater-shaped shield of the Royal Arms ensigned with an Imperial Crown. The combination of the shape of this shield together with the position of the crown caused this coin to be known as the "spade guinea". In the reign of George IV the Royal Crest of England first appears on the shilling. On George IV's half-crown is a shield of the Royal Arms surmounted by a crowned Royal helm, with mantling suspended from it on either side of the shield and a motto scroll below.

From the commencement of the reign of King George VI a proportion of shillings have been struck with the Scottish Royal Crest on the reverse. These are the first Scottish coins to be minted since 1707.

Our present coins are notable for the armorial excellence of the design, and it is worth comparing them with earlier and more insipid coins bearing similar devices.

Small heraldic charges were used for various purposes on the mediaeval coins. The term "mint-mark" is freely applied to some of them, and includes two principal varieties: an "Initial mark", which shows where the inscription on a coin starts, and a "privy mark", the purpose of which is uncertain, but which may denote the workman responsible for striking the coin. Initial marks include crosses, fleurs-de-lis, crowns, roses, cinqfoils, cross-crosslets, boars' heads, dragons, tuns, suns, annulets and lions. The boar's head and the dragon were the respective badges of Richard III and Henry VII and were used by them. Privy marks comprise annulets, mullets, broken letters, etc., which are placed in various parts of the design. A groat of Henry VI, for instance, has annulets by the neck on the obverse and in two of the angles of the cross on the reverse.

The Archbishops of Canterbury and York had a mediaeval right of coinage, and from the reign of King Edward I the Archbishop of York distinguished his "York" pennies by a quatrefoil in the centre of the cross on the reverse. On the obverse of groats struck by Edward III and Edward IV the background behind the head of the King is semé of trefoils. This raises the interesting question as to whether the trefoil was an English as well as a Scottish and Irish badge. Or, alternatively, whether it was originally merely a repetition of the three-roundel design on the reverse of the coinage. A third possibility is that the three roundels are or became a conventional representation of a trefoil. (It may be that some significance was attached to the roundel. It is first seen on Offa's silver penny. The banner which the Pope presented to William the Conqueror for the invasion of England incorporates a cross patée between four roundels—another approximation, incidentally, to the arms of Jerusalem.) Trefoils first appeared on the Scottish Great Seal at about the same time that the design incorporating the three roundels was standardised on the English penny.

Coins are an even bigger study than seals, and a wealth of literature has been written about them. It is not the purpose of this brief outline to replace, or even to supplement, any of that literature, but rather to divert attention to another of the numerous avenues which the student of heraldry may explore.

Chapter XIX

ARMORIAL AUTHORITIES

THERE is no record of heralds in Great Britain before the reign of Edward I, but they are mentioned in French history a hundred years earlier. They were originally professional proclaimers and criers, and are particularly mentioned in connection with tournaments, which seem to have been their especial province. Some were attached to the great lords and followed them from one jousting contest to another; whilst others led a nomad, and frequently poverty-stricken, life, wandering from court to court and from tournament to tournament. It was a profession in which there were many grades, varying from wealth and comfort to impecunious vagrancy. The nature of a herald's duties entailed a very detailed knowledge of armory and it was almost a point of honour to be able to recognise any arms he saw. The armorial knowledge of the heralds led to their being increasingly entrusted with the organisation of tournaments, until eventually they became completely responsible for their conduct. Another employment was that of messenger, and the heralds travelled between the courts of Europe as ambassadors in war and peace. The first named herald in England was Carlisle, who was created by Edward III, probably in 1327 when he passed near to the town of Carlisle during the Scottish campaign of that year. In 1338 Carlisle Herald is mentioned as bringing letters to England from the King of Spain and information concerning a state of war which had arisen on the Continent between the vassals of the King of England and those of the King of France.

The multiplication of heralds led to the appointment of one of their number as King of Heralds, or, as he later came to be called, King of Arms, who presided over all the heralds of a kingdom or of a province. As yet, however, the heralds had no jurisdiction over arms or any connection with their grant.

Arms, as we have already seen, were a gradual growth, of which the first indications appear in the early part of the twelfth century. When Geoffrey Plantagenet, Count of Anjou, was knighted by King Henry I of England, on the occasion of his marriage to the King's daughter, Maud, a shield charged with six gold lioncels was hung about his neck. His bastard grandson, William Longespée, Earl of Salisbury, bore these same arms, and they appear, as we have already seen, on the seal of Ela Basset. Ralph, Count of Vermandois, 1116 to 1152, bore a chequy shield.

The 1136-38 seal of his nephew Waleran, Count of Meulan and Lord of Worcester, shows these same chequers on the shield, lance flag and bardings of the horse. On his seal of 1141-42 the same arms appear again on shield, surcoat and helm. The well-known chevrons of Clare are first seen on a seal of 1141-46. These early arms were, of course, adopted by the free choice of their owners (except that Geoffrey Plantagenet may perhaps claim the first Royal grant). The only difference between them and previous devices was that they became hereditary. Arms were generally assumed throughout the thirteenth and fourteenth centuries, though it was considered a greater honour to have them by grant of the Sovereign. By the middle of the thirteenth century there is a recognised system of adoption of arms and very few instances of the same coat being borne by two individuals. By the end of the century there appears to have been a recognition of property in arms, and by the laws of the fourteenth century a man had a right to assume a distinctive coat of arms at his own hand and to obtain redress against any other person who should subsequently use the same arms.

Disputes as to the ownership of arms were not infrequent, and they appear to have been decided either by the Sovereign himself or by the Constable and Marshal acting for him. The offices of Constable and Marshal date from the reign of Henry I. They were primarily military officers, but they had duties at the King's Court as well. A military court presided over by the Constable and Marshal existed in the time of Edward I and probably earlier. Its precise jurisdiction is doubtful, but it certainly adjudicated disputes as to the ownership of arms. Disputes which were not easily settled by adjudication or arbitration were sometimes decided by combat. The most famous instance of this resulted from the rival claims in 1389 of the houses of Carminow, Scrope and Grosvenor to the arms, "Azure, a bend or". The contest between Carminow and Scrope was indecisive and both were allowed to retain the arms, which they still do. Scrope, however, defeated Grosvenor, who was directed to difference his arms with a bordure argent. Grosvenor appealed to the King, who ordered him to give up the arms. Grosvenor finally assumed "Azure, a garb or", part of the arms of the Earls of Chester, to whom he was related by descent.

The first real attempt to bring the acquirement of arms under proper control was made by King Henry V in 1417. In Letters Patent to the Sheriffs of the counties of Hampshire, Sussex, Wiltshire and Dorsetshire, the King stated that in recent expeditions overseas many persons had assumed arms which neither they nor their ancestors had previously used. He directed proclamation to be made forbidding the assumption of arms unless a person had them by ancestral right or by grant of some person having authority to do so; and further that all, except those who had borne arms at Agincourt, should on a certain day declare their arms and how they had obtained them. It is conjectured that this exemption of men who had fought at Agincourt was in Shakespeare's mind when he attributed the following words to the King:

> "We few, we happy few, we band of brothers;
> For he to-day that sheds his blood with me
> Shall be my brother; be he ne'er so base,
> This day shall gentle his condition."

In the same year Henry V created the new office of Garter Principal King of Arms of Englishmen; and his brother, Thomas of Lancaster, Duke of Clarence, who was Constable of the Army, reorganised the armorial system to give effect to the King's decrees. His "Ordinances" made Garter King of Arms the Sovereign of the Office of Arms; and authorised Garter Kings of Arms generally and the other Kings of Arms in their provinces to register all arms in use with the names of their owners, and to grant arms with proper differences to applicants. The effect of the King's orders and the Duke of Clarence's Ordinances was that no Englishmen henceforth had the right to assume arms, and all arms which had been assumed in the past had to be recorded if they were to remain valid.

In 1483 King Richard III made a further improvement in the heraldic organisation by the foundation of the College of Arms, which was incorporated by Royal Charter. Amongst the duties of the new College were the regulation of the bearing of arms, the granting of arms to persons considered worthy to bear them, and the prevention of the unauthorised assumption of arms.

In order to ensure that all arms were properly recorded and that unauthorised arms were not being used, a system of visitations was instituted. The Crown would issue Letters Patent notifying mayors, sheriffs, etc., that Clarenceux King of Arms or Norroy King of Arms, according to whether the area concerned was south or north of the River Trent, would shortly make a visitation in his province to correct arms unlawfully borne and to enter those borne lawfully. It is not known exactly when the first of these visitations took place, but they became fairly frequent between the years 1530 and 1686; the last of them occurring in the latter year.

A certain amount of confusion was caused through Garter's indefinite jurisdiction, and in 1673 it was laid down that all Patents should be issued by the three Kings of Arms jointly, and in no case without first obtaining the authority of the Earl Marshal. In 1680 this ruling was modified so that Garter and Clarenceux dealt with England south of the Trent, whilst Garter and Norroy dealt with that part of England which lay to the north of it.

Since the ruling of 1673 all Patents have been recorded in a single series by the College of Arms as a Corporation. In the case of Patents prior to 1673 it is necessary to rely on the dockets kept by the individual Kings of Arms, on the Patents themselves and on copies subsequently made. Patents may be in respect of entirely new grants of arms, they may be issued in confirmation of a right which was previously considered uncertain or they may be exemplifications under Royal licence authorising the transfer of arms from one family to another.

The heraldic authorities in the United Kingdom are now as follows:

1. *The United Kingdom (except Scotland).*

The head of the College of Arms is the Earl Marshal. This office is held of hereditary right by the Dukes of Norfolk in virtue of Letters Patent issued by Charles II in 1672. Garter King of Arms, who is immediately attached to the order of that name, is the Principal King of Arms. Clarenceux King of Arms is responsible for England south of the River Trent and Wales. England north of the River Trent has, since mediaeval times, been the province of Norroy King of Arms. Until 1943 heraldic affairs for the whole of Ireland were dealt with by Ulster King of Arms. In that year, however, the Government of Eire took over the Ulster Office in Dublin Castle and appointed a Chief Herald of Ireland. In consequence Norroy King of Arms has had his title changed to Norroy and Ulster, and becomes responsible for Northern Ireland, which is, of course, part of the United Kingdom. Northern Ireland is now, therefore, under the jurisdiction of the Earl Marshal of England, which it never was before. There are six English heralds: Chester, Windsor, Lancaster, York, Richmond and Somerset. There are four pursuivants, the lowest degree of officers of arms: Rouge Croix (so called from the red cross of St. George), Blue Mantle (named after the blue mantle of France assumed by Edward III), Rouge Dragon (from Henry VIII's supporter) and Portcullis (after Henry VIII's badge of that name).

2. *Scotland.*

Lyon King of Arms is the chief heraldic authority in Scotland. He is not under the control of the Earl Marshal of England. His Court is one of the Scottish judicatures and has considerable powers, unlike the Court of the Earl Marshal, which no longer sits. Under an Act of 1592 Lyon King of Arms can escheat to the Sovereign all goods unlawfully displaying arms. For each offence contravening the Act a fine of £100

Scots can be imposed, or imprisonment during the pleasure of the Lord Lyon. The numbers of heralds and pursuivants are now fixed at three of each. The heralds' titles at present in use are Marchmont, Rothesay and Albany; and those of the pursuivants are Unicorn, Falkland and Carrick.

THE RIGHT TO BEAR ARMS

The position in the United Kingdom is that no arms are valid unless they have been the subject of a grant or a confirmation by the Officers of Arms, to whom the Sovereign has delegated control of armory. As we have seen, arms in early days were generally selected and assumed without reference to any authority, and the laws of the fourteenth century recognised and protected this practice. Henry V's decree of 1417 forbade the assumption of arms, and from the wording of his proclamation it appears that arms were already more often granted than assumed. The primary purpose of the visitations was to record and confirm all the arms which were in use but which had not been the subject of a grant. Many people are under the impression that if their ancestors assumed arms in mediaeval times, and these arms were never recorded, they are entitled to bear them. This is not the case. All arms must have been recorded and the right to them confirmed. If this has not been done there is nothing to stop them being legally granted to somebody else. Not only must arms have been confirmed, but they must be recorded for each generation. If a family thinks itself entitled to an ancient coat of arms, the first thing to find out is whether the arms were ever either granted to or confirmed as being rightly in the possession of an ancestor. The second requirement is to prove descent from that ancestor, or supposed ancestor. If the arms required have never been granted or recorded at one of the visitations, then a fresh grant of arms will be necessary. Provided that the arms which the family have been using have not been granted to somebody else and that they comply with the laws of armory, they would probably be granted.

In Scotland, of course, all younger members in each generation of a family only have the right to petition the Lord Lyon for differenced versions of their father's arms. These differenced arms are "matriculated" in the Lyon Register in the petitioner's name. It would be quite wrong, therefore, for a younger son to use his father's arms undifferenced.

In Ireland the visitations were infrequent and no complete record of the arms in use was ever made. On account of this, Ulster King of Arms possessed the power of granting confirmation of arms to families which had been using the same arms for at least three generations or before 1800. This power is now presumably held by Norroy and Ulster

King of Arms in respect of Northern Ireland. In the Republic of Ireland the Chief Herald has carried on the practice of Ulster.

For a non-armigerous person to obtain arms it is necessary to petition for a grant. Particulars of birth, ancestry and profession will be required. If the applicant comes within the jurisdiction of the College of Arms, one of the Officers of Arms will conduct the case, and he will prepare a "memorial" (or petition) and send it to the applicant for signature. (In Scotland and the Republic of Ireland printed forms are used instead of memorials.) The College of Arms will then decide on the limitations of the grant, that is, to what branches and descendants of the family it is to apply. The fees now have to be paid. The College of Arms requires £105 for an English grant of arms and £66 for an Irish one. The fees charged by the Lyon Office and by Dublin Castle are lower, since, unlike the College of Arms, the salaries are paid by the State. After the payment of the fees the memorial is sent to the Earl Marshal. If he approves, he issues a warrant authorising the College of Arms to make the grant. If the design of the new arms has not yet been decided it will now be discussed. The Patent will then be drawn up. This is carried out in illuminated work on vellum with a painting of the arms in the corner, and it is signed and sealed by Garter King of Arms and by one of the other two Kings of Arms.

There are no armorial authorities in the British Dominions or the Colonies. British subjects overseas who require a grant of arms should apply to the College of Arms, unless they are of Scottish descent, when they may prefer to petition the Lord Lyon. Persons who are not of British nationality may apply to the College of Arms for a grant of arms. If authorised by the Earl Marshal they are termed "Honorary Armorial Bearings", though there is no practical difference between these and ordinary grants.

If an armigerous person becomes domiciled in a country which is subject to an armorial authority other than the one from which his arms were obtained, he should record them with that authority. For instance, an Englishman who settles in Scotland should apply for matriculation of his arms in the Lyon Register. In granting a warrant for matriculation the Lord Lyon will difference them so far as Scots law requires.

Chapter XX

THE PRACTICAL USE OF ARMS

"It is in and through symbols that man consciously or unconsciously lives, moves and has his being. Those ages, moreover, are accounted the noblest which can best recognise symbolical worth and prize it at the highest."
—CARLYLE.

WE are surrounded by the emblems of armory. The national flags display the banners of our country's patron saints. Our coins bear the Royal Arms and badges. Letters from Government departments are headed by a Royal badge, and those from county and borough councils frequently bear the civic arms. The inns of England have ancient badges for their signs. Stained-glass windows, tombs and memorials in our cathedrals and churches are adorned with family arms. The uniforms, badges and colours of our fighting forces are heraldic. And, of course, the great State occasions are rich in armory and armorial tradition.

In view of this almost universal love of symbols, it is surprising that the desire to possess a personal device and a knowledge of the rules governing its use is not more widespread. New arms are constantly being granted, but on the other hand there must be many families who could prove a right to ancient arms the very existence of which they have forgotten. Other families use a crest to which they may very likely be entitled, but they have no knowledge of the much more important arms to which the crest is attached, or indeed that a crest can have no existence without arms. Still others use bogus arms which may very well have originated in a piece of armorial table-ware acquired in a curiosity shop. Most heraldic errors are committed through ignorance and not from any deliberate pretence to the legitimate ownership of unauthorised achievements, and many of them may be forgiven for the love of heraldry to which they bear witness.

Personal armorial bearings have been put to many uses in the past, and some of these are summarised below with comments on their modern application.

1. Stonework

Arms can frequently be seen carved on the great houses of England and their stone gateways. One of the most famous examples is provided by the arms of Cardinal Wolsey, which are carved on Hampton Court

PLATE 26

BOOKPLATES

Fig. 1

Argent, three bars gules; overall, on a pile ermine, above two quills in saltire of the field, the points in base, three martlets sable; in the dexter chief the canton of a baronet.

Crest: *A griffin sejant reguardant sable, the dexter fore foot resting on an escarbuncle argent.*

Fig. 2

Azure, a chevron ermine between three demi cobras erect proper; on a chief embattled or, three pellets.

Crest: *A demi cobra as in the arms.*

The achievement displays the circlet and badge of the Most Distinguished Order of Saint Michael and Saint George.

Fig. 3

Argent, three boars' heads couped Scottish fashion sable.

Crest: *A boar's head as in the arms.*

The Esquire's helm shown is the fifteenth century jousting helm.

Fig. 4

Argent, a lion rampant gules between three pheons sable.

Crest: *A sheaf of arrows, the points downwards, one in pale and two in saltire tied with a riband argent.*

Supporters: *Dexter a wyvern, sinister a lion ducally crowned.*

The coronet of an earl is shown above the shield.

· VIVERE · VIRTUTE ·

William E. Berry.

Colonel
Frank Wall,
C.M.G.

RUSSELL BARTON

Seymour William Arthur
John Egerton
Earl of Wilton

PLATE 27

BOOKPLATES

USE OF CRESTS WITHOUT THE ARMS

Fig. 1

A stag lodged with a non-armorial design.

Fig 2

A cock.

Fig. 3

A wyvern and a lion passant guardant— the position known in early days as "leopard".

Fig. 4

A sheaf of arrows.

J·F·GALLAND

WAUTHIER

COMMIT THY WORK TO GOD

William Noble Sinclair

ESSE QUAM VIDERI

M.H.G.P.Croft

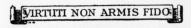

VIRTUTI NON ARMIS FIDO

Stephen Loftus Egerton

Palace. Few in these days can afford to live in large country houses, and arms on the same scale adorning the wall of a suburban villa would, of course, look absurd. But there is plenty of scope for an achievement of the right scale for the smallest house, its design depending on the type and architecture of the building.

2. *Ironwork*

Arms have often been very effectively embodied in the design of wrought-iron gateways. Cast-iron fire-backs have been another favourite method of displaying arms; and amongst the smaller articles some beautiful armorial designs have been produced on door plates and knockers. All these are suitable for present-day use.

3. *Furniture, Panelling, etc.*

Furniture, panelling, chimney pieces and other woodwork have been carved with many attractive heraldic designs. An oak-panelled room is very suitable for displaying shields of arms. The arms of all a family's connections, for instance, may be carved round the room: one shield to each panel. Dining-room chair-backs provide another example of suitable furniture for armorial carving.

4. *Silver and Ornamental Boxes, etc.*

Household silver is often engraved with armorial emblems. A generation ago this was probably the commonest way of displaying family crests. Unfortunately it was only the crest that was normally engraved, and this is one of the reasons why so many arms have been forgotten and why the crest has acquired such an exaggerated importance. Small boxes and other similar ornaments of various materials are often seen decorated with heraldic designs, and some of the best heraldic art has been executed on these little objects. Silver, table ornaments, dressing-table sets, etc., are all obviously suitable articles to bear an achievement of arms.

5. *China, Glass, Earthenware, etc.*

Some of the most beautiful emblazoning of arms has been done on china, and there are some lovely examples of this work to be seen in the heraldic museum in Dublin Castle. China is particularly suitable for displaying delicate colouring to the best advantage. Glass beakers, earthenware beer-mugs and other table-ware have also provided some of the finest armorial work.

6. *Bookplates and Notepaper*

An engraved bookplate is a very popular method of depicting arms. It provides endless scope for the exercise of armorial art, it adds to the beauty of any book, it is personal and it is reasonably inexpensive. Armorial bookplates probably originated with the printers' devices of the fifteenth century. Notepaper is probably the most popular and most common medium of all for the display of arms. The achievement, or a portion of it, is cut on a die and stamped on the head of the paper. Again, the crest alone is all too often used. The full achievement is generally preferable, but if any part of it is to be used alone it should be the shield of arms, which is the basis of the whole thing.

7. *Seals*

Seals are no longer part of a man's essential equipment, but the small seal or signet ring is still very much used. Its diminutive size is an inducement to engrave it with a crest only, but on even the smallest signet a shield of arms can generally be quite clearly cut, provided that no quarterings are included.

8. *Garments*

In mediaeval times the knight's surcoat or jupon was embroidered with his arms, and his lady wore a dress or mantle on which she displayed her husband's arms alone or else impaled with her own paternal arms. Officers of arms at the present time, of course, wear tabards embroidered with the arms of the Sovereign. Modern dress does not give very much scope for the display of arms. They can, however, be knitted into pull-overs, embroidered on the pockets of blazers and embodied in the design of ladies' frocks and evening capes.

There are many other articles and materials on which arms may be suitably depicted, including hearth-rugs, tapestry fire-screens, stained-glass windows, decorated ceilings, doors of cars and carriages, personal banners and table mats. The student will be able to think of several others.

DESIGN

Design has been mentioned already in connection with various parts of the achievement, so that much of what follows is a repetition of matter included in earlier chapters. First of all it is emphasised again that it is desirable, wherever space and the nature of article and material permit, to use the full achievement. For the average person this includes shield, helm, mantling, crest and, possibly, motto. Proportions are important. The height of the helm and crest together should be at least the same as the height of the shield, and some authorities allot one-third of the height of the achievement each to helm, crest and shield as the ideal proportions. The shield should be an artistic shape, and the so-called

PLATE 28

BOOKPLATES

Fig. 1

Sable, on a chevron between three hinds trippant argent, three annulets of the field.

Crest: *A stag trippant the dexter fore foot resting on an escutcheon argent.*

Fig. 2

Azure, on a fess between three fetterlocks argent a mullet sable, within a bordure per pale or and of the second.

Crest: *An arm embowed in armour, the hand in a gauntlet grasping a dagger the point to the dexter proper.*

The Esquire's helm is a great helm.

Fig. 3

A non-armorial bookplate showing a dragon rampant.

Fig. 4

Argent, a chevron between three boars' heads couped Scottish fashion sable; on a chief vert, three bezants.

Crest: *A falcon close belled proper.*

A. RANSFORD COLLETT

WARDELL

heater shield is as attractive as any for arms of a single coat. This is drawn as follows:

Draw a line *AB*, the required width of the shield. With the point of the compass on *A* and the pencil on *B*, describe the arc of a circle downwards. With the compass point on *B* and the pencil on *A*, describe another arc downwards to intersect the first. These two intersecting arcs will give the boundary of the lower part of the shield. Now on *A* and *B* erect two perpendicular lines each equal to one-third of *AB*. Join them at the top, and the heater shield is complete.

The charges should be so drawn that they fill the shield without obscuring the field. Animals should look heraldic, and lions and other savage beasts should look savage and full of life. It is not in the least necessary that they should be an accurate portrayal of the natural animal. The angle of a chevron should not be greater than a right angle and its apex should reach as near to the honour point as possible without cramping the charges unduly. Hatching, to represent the tinctures, should be employed only if its use does not deaden the design or if it is necessary to indicate the colours for some particular reason. A heater shield is most effectively represented couché, that is, suspended from the sinister chief.

The helm should be one that a man could wear and preferably a representation of a type that was actually worn. Helm and shield should not belong to different periods. If the position rule of helmets is observed, the helm should be twisted slightly, if necessary, one way and the crest the other, to avoid as far as possible the unpleasant combination of, for instance, a lion passant on an affronté helm.

The mantling is a great aid to the composition of the whole achievement and its most effective arrangement requires considerable thought. It can either be shown as a piece of uncut drapery or blown into jagged patterns of tongue-shaped pieces.

A wreath should look, as it is meant to be, a piece of soft twisted material wound round the helm. The crest should appear to be firmly attached to the helm and not balanced precariously on its apex.

PLATE 29

Ex Libris
Frank Stanley Service

Ex libris
Douglas Service

THE BOOKPLATES OF A FATHER (LEFT) AND ELDEST SON

These show the different interpretation by two Herald Painters of the same marshalling.

THE BOOKPLATE OF A YOUNGER SON OF
THE SAME FAMILY

It will be seen that Lyon has differenced the Arms for cadency by the addition of a border, thus following Stoddart's scheme, which is set out in plate 11 and which is commonly used in Scotland today.

Appendix A

INSIGNIA WHICH SHOULD ACCOMPANY SHIELDS OF ARMS IN THE ROMAN CATHOLIC CHURCH

Degree	Colour of Ecclesiastical Hat	Number and Colour of Tassels on each side	Other Insignia	Remarks
1. *Cardinal*	Red	15 Red	According to ecclesiastical rank, i.e. archbishop, bishop, etc.	Cardinals may not use any other insignia or accessories except the crosses of the Orders of Malta and of the Holy Sepulchre.
2. *Patriarch and Primate*	Green	15 Green	A cross with two bars in pale behind the shield. Residential patriarchs and primates may surround their shields with the pallium (In British practice the pallium generally appears as a charge in the arms of the primatial or archi-episcopal see)	No insignia of temporal dignity or nobility are now allowed, even any which may belong to the see. The rules are now the same as for cardinals

3. *Archbishop not a Primate*	Green	10 Green	As for patriarchs	As for patriarchs
4. *Bishop*	Green	6 Green	A cross with a single bar in pale behind the shield. If the pallium is possessed by special concession it may be used as above	As for patriarchs
5. *Abbot and Prelate "Nullius"*	Green	6 Green	A mitre above the shield and a crozier in pale behind the shield with a veil attached to it	There is no specific order preventing the use of temporal insignia by these and lesser dignitaries, but they should, nevertheless, abide by the same rules as the higher prelate
6. (a) *Abbot and Provost who receive abbatial benediction*	Black	6 Black	As above	
(b) *Superiors and general provincial of most of the religious Orders and Congregations, their Vicars, and some others of similar position*				
(c) *Titular Apostolic Protonotaries*				
(d) *Vicars general and capitular and any others possessing similar privileges*				
(e) *Canons of certain Chapters*				

Appendix A (continued)

INSIGNIA WHICH SHOULD ACCOMPANY SHIELDS OF ARMS IN THE ROMAN CATHOLIC CHURCH (*continued*)

Degree	Colour of Ecclesiastical Hat	Number and Colour of Tassels on each side	Other Insignia	Remarks
7. *Prelate "di Fiochetto"* (The Vice-Camerlingue of the Holy Roman Church, the Auditor General, the Treasurer General of the Apostolic Chamber and the Majordomo of His Holiness)	Violet	10 Red		Some of these prelates are often archbishops, in which case they use archiepiscopal insignia
8. *Apostolic Protonotary* (except titular) This includes: (a) Apostolic Protonotaries "de numero Participantium" (b) Assessors and Secretaries of the Sacred Roman Congregations (c) The Master of His Holiness' Chamber (d) The Secretary of the Apostolic Signature (e) The Dean of the Roman Rota	Violet	6 Red	No other	

(f) The Deputy of the Secretary of State				
(g) The Vicars, Prefects and Administrators Apostolic during their term of office				
(h) Supernumerary Apostolic Protonotaries				
(i) Apostolic Protonotaries "ad instar Participantium"				
9. *Domestic Prelate* This includes: (a) The Auditors of the Sacred Roman Rota (b) The Clerks of the Apostolic Chamber (c) The Voters of the Apostolic Signature (d) The Confirmed Members of the three Colleges of the Prelature (e) The Referenders of the Apostolic Signature (f) All domestic Prelates nominated by apostolic brief	Violet	6 Violet	No other	
10. *Privy Chamberlain and Privy Chaplain to His Holiness*	Black	6 Violet	No other	These insignia are not firm, as the matter has not yet been decided

Appendix A (continued)

INSIGNIA WHICH SHOULD ACCOMPANY SHIELDS OF ARMS IN THE ROMAN CATHOLIC CHURCH (continued)

Degree	Colour of Ecclesiastical Hat	Number and Colour of Tassels on each side	Other Insignia	Remarks
11. Canon				
(a) Canons Ordinary	Black	3 Black	No other	
(b) Canons of Chapters having privileges of Protonotaries Apostolic	Violet	6 Red	No other	
(c) Canons of Chapters having privileges of Domestic Prelates	Violet	6 Violet	No other	
(d) Canons of Chapters having privileges of "Privy Chamberlains"	Black	6 Violet	No other	Not yet firm
(e) Canons of Chapters privileged to use the mitre	Black	3 Black	A mitre above the shield	
(f) Canons of Chapters possessing the collective title of count or baron	Black	3 Black	The coronet of a count or baron above the shield	
12. Dean, Minor, Superior, Archpriest, Diocesan Functionary, etc.	Black	2 Black	No other	This is not firm, but is a matter of custom or propriety

	Black	I Black	No other	
13. *Priest*				
14. *Abbess*	None	None	A crozier with a veil attached in pale behind the shield. A rosary encircling the shield	The crozier is only used by those abbesses who have the right to carry it on certain official occasions in the convent and in processions. All members of religious orders have the right to encircle their shield with a rosary

Appendix B

BIBLIOGRAPHY

A. C. Fox-Davies . . . . A Complete Guide to Heraldry
Ecclesiastical Heraldry (Catholic Encyclopedia)

V. Wheeler-Holohan . . Boutell's Manual of Heraldry
A Manual of Flags

G. W. Eve . . . . Heraldry as Art

J. Woodward and G. Burnett . A Treatise on Heraldry

J. Woodward . . . . Ecclesiastical Heraldry

Sir Christopher and Adrian
Lynch-Robinson . . . Intelligible Heraldry

J. Foster . . . . . Some Feudal Coats of Arms

C. W. Scott-Giles . . . The Romance of Heraldry
Civic Heraldry

Sir F. J. Grant . . . . Manual of Heraldry

Porny . . . . . The Elements of Heraldry, 1771

J. Vinycomb . . . . Fictitious Creatures in Art

Debrett . . . . . Peerage of the United Kingdom

Sir William Dugdale . . The Antient Usage in Bearing Arms, 1682

Douglas Jerrold . . . An Introduction to the History of England

Colonel L. I. Cowper, O.B.E., D.L. The King's Own. The Story of a Royal Regiment

J. R. Planché . . . . The Pursuivant at Arms, 1851

J. H. Stevenson . . . Heraldry in Scotland

John Guillim . . . . A Display of Heraldry, 1611

Harold Pereira (Imperial Chemical Industries) . . . The Colour of Chivalry

Guy Cadogan Rothery . . The A B C of Heraldry

Innes of Learney . . . Scots Heraldry

Walter de Gray Birch . . Seals

J. Harvey Bloom . . . English Seals

A. Wagner . . . . Heraldry in England
Historic Heraldry of Britain
Heralds and Heraldry in the Middle Ages

BURKE	General Armory
JAMES DALLAWAY . . .	Inquiries into the Origin and Progress of Heraldry in England
E. F. DORLING	Leopards of England
J. E. CUSSANS	The Handbook of Heraldry
E. J. JONES	Mediaeval Heraldry
CHARLES A. H. FRANKLIN . .	The Bearing of Coat Armour by Ladies
HERBERT COLE	Heraldry and Floral Forms on Decoration
Mgr. BRUNO BERNARD HEIM .	Coutumes et Droits Héraldiques de L'Eglise
J. G. MILNE, C. H. V. SUTHERLAND and J. D. A. THOMPSON . .	Coin Collecting
Rear-Admiral G. H. PREBLE, U.S.N.	History of the Flag of the United States of America and Other National Flags
THE HERALDRY SOCIETY . .	The Coat of Arms

INDEX

INDEX